THE GLORIES OF
SALISBURY CATHEDRAL

Salisbury Cathedral: spire and transepts from the south.

THE GLORIES OF
SALISBURY
CATHEDRAL

By JEFFREY TRUBY

Photographs by
A. W. KERR

WINCHESTER PUBLICATIONS LIMITED
16 MADDOX STREET LONDON W.1

First published in mcmxlviii by
Winchester Publications Limited
16 Maddox Street, London, W.1.

The Publishers desire to acknowledge their obligation
to the Dean and Chapter of Salisbury Cathedral
who granted permission for photographs to be taken.

MADE AND PRINTED IN GREAT BRITAIN BY L. T. A. ROBINSON, LTD., LONDON, S.W.9

CONTENTS

The Plates are on pages 38—113. There is a List of the Plates on pages 36 and 37, and a Glossary of Architectural and Ecclesiastical Terms on page 114.

I

Perfect Gothic

SEVEN hundred years have passed since Richard le Poore began to build his Cathedral in the Wiltshire meadows. The centuries that have worn empires away and eroded the cliffs, that have covered ancient cities with sand and clothed new towns with grime and squalor, have done little more to the great church of Salisbury than to etch its lineaments with a softer beauty and to deepen its regard in the minds of men.

It was neither perversity nor pride that made Richard le Poore choose so unlikely a site. It is doubtful if he foresaw that the prehistoric fortress that had been the seat of his predecessors would crumble into dust and its name be remembered only by scholars. There is no reason to suppose that he set out to replace it by a spacious new city, which would be flourishing still when men had learned to make their voices heard from continent to continent, to soar above the earth and to sail under the seas. He planned simply to build a church. That was all. He intended to build a church to the glory of God, and because he planned with genius the church came to be a glory in stone. Because he lived at a time when imagination was escaping from the trammels of the Dark Ages, he was helped by masons who could respond to his own daring, masons eager to do with their materials things that had never been done before, masons who had learned with mallet and chisel to become master artists. Vision and circumstance combined to give the building a coherence possessed by no other cathedral in the land, and to fashion it into a supreme example of Early English architecture.

Richard le Poore was not the first to feel that Old Sarum was an unworthy seat for a bishop. It was an earthen fort, no less rough in the twelfth century than in the pagan times when religion had its centre in the mysterious circle of Stonehenge. From its eminence as a Celtic stronghold, it had probably fallen into disuse during the Roman occupation, becoming important again during the Anglo-Saxon invasions. When the country was converted to Christianity the early bishops took up residence in open villages, and the diocese of Wiltshire was for long administered from the village of Ramsbury. But wars continued, open towns were sacked, and in the year 1075 Wiltshire's Bishop Herman obeyed the king's order to remove to Sarum. Herman, a Fleming by birth and one of Edward the Confessor's chaplains, at once began to build a cathedral within the fortress.

It was a discouraging task. The fortress was small, cramped, filthy, fever-ridden and The walls were so high that the crowded dwellings were gloomy even in high enough in winter to keep out the miserable cold of the windswept ough to have held the mint of Canute and Edward the Confessor, the fortress yet lacked an adequate water supply. The aged Bishop Herman began to map out the Cathedral but died within two years. His successor, known to later generations as St. Osmund, inherited the task. The building was consecrated in 1092. Two days later, it was struck by lightning and the roof destroyed. Osmund patiently repaired the damage and endowed a chapter consisting of the dean, precentor, chancellor, treasurer and thirty-two canons. Other bishops followed him.

Towards the end of the twelfth century came Herbert le Poore, illegitimate son of a bishop, more skilful with accounts than learned in theology and only a deacon when elected to the see of Sarum. But he was no time-server. With Hugh of Lincoln he raised a campaign against the oppressive taxation of Richard I. He suffered persecution and insult in consequence, and once had to fly to Scotland to preserve his liberty. It was he who first revolted against the drunken licentiousness of the mercenaries who garrisoned the fortress. Somehow he obtained the King's permission to remove the see, though the turbulence of the times prevented him from carrying out his resolve.

On his death in 1217 he was succeeded by his brother Richard, illegitimate like himself but of greater learning, and until then Bishop of Chichester. Directly Richard had established his new episcopate, he began to seek a site outside the overcrowded fortress. He did not want to go beyond the great plain of Salisbury, or even outside his own episcopal estate. He selected a site on the edge of his lands known as Myrfield. Probably he selected it because it was on the boundary of three ancient parishes, was only two miles to the south of Old Sarum, and was situated near a good road. That the land was marshy seemed to him of no importance. He had confidence in his ability to overcome difficulties. A mission was despatched to Rome. Pope Honorius III issued a bull of assent on March 29, 1219. By November of the same year a temporary church had been built, and the bishop and chapter left Old Sarum with relief. Within a few months the designs for the new and magnificent Cathedral were complete; on April 28, 1220, a crowd gathered to witness the beginning of its translation from drawings to stone.

Barefoot, according to custom, the bishop led the procession of clergy and noblemen from a service in the temporary church to the chosen site. Many of the barons were away fighting in the Welsh Marches, and statesmen were kept preoccupied in London. But William Longespee, Earl of Sarum, the foremost of peers and bravest of warriors, was among those who heard Richard le Poore's sermon in the open air. The bishop laid three foundation stones: one in the name of the Pope, the second in the name of the Archbishop of Canterbury, the third in his own. Then followed the laying of stones by Longespee, his wife, and several barons. The Cathedral's history had begun.

It was the beginning, too, of the city of Salisbury. The civil population of Old Sarum soon left the dark fortress to join the masons in the riverside meadows, so that Bishop le Poore found himself with a fair-sized population to house. Again he acted promptly. He set architects and master craftsmen to plan a town of straight streets and square blocks of dwellings all of much the same size. This was to be a town that would be in harmony with the Cathedral, and which in design and spaciousness would be unlike most other English towns.

` Money flowed in. The bishop, watching block being added to block, spent his private fortune without stint. The barons returning from the Welsh wars gave subscriptions. The building of the Cathedral went on with a speed remarkable for the times. Within five years divine service was celebrated in the choir. In the autumn of 1225 three altars were consecrated by three prelates—Stephen Langton, Archbishop of Canterbury, the Archbishop of Dublin, and Richard le Poore. On the next day, September 29, the Cathedral was consecrated in the presence of the papal nuncio and a great congregation to whom Langton preached.

A month later, Henry III and his justiciar, Hubert de Burgh, came with rich presents; in December they returned with a further royal gift of a ruby, a gold cup and silk. In the following Spring William Longespee, Earl of Sarum, died and was buried in the new cathedral, and the bones of St. Osmund and others were brought from Old Sarum. Stone from the old cathedral helped in the building of the new. The dean, the precentor Roger, later to be Bishop of Bath and Wells, the treasurer who was to become Archbishop of Canterbury, the Canon Elias de Derham who may have been the chief clerk of works or master builder—these men were fired by the bishop's zeal. In 1228, Richard le Poore was translated to Durham. One of his last acts in English history was to witness Henry III's confirmation of Magna Carta. When he died he was buried neither in Durham nor Salisbury but in a little Cistercian nunnery which he had endowed.

Still the building went on. A new bishop came and worked steadfastly for eighteen years. Then came another, "better versed in the laws of the realm than those of God". But he, too, pressed forward the task begun by Richard le Poore. Under the next bishop, Giles de Bridport, the main building was finished and in 1258 another solemn consecration ceremony was held. The west front, the tower and spire were to be added later. The cloisters were probably designed about the year 1260 and completed after eighty years, and the chapter house appears to date from 1270 or 1280. None the less, the whole of the Cathedral could be used for the services and ceremonies of the Church by 1258, less than forty years after the foundation stones were laid. That was an exceptionally short period for so great an achievement. Moreover, the speed was partly responsible for the greatness of the work, since it ensured that in this Cathedral there should be no disparity of style.

Salisbury has other advantages. It is splendid of approach. There are some great churches that, for all the dignity of their venerable age, still seem alien in their surroundings, as if they had been transported entire from some Continental land. There are others that must be sought for through devious streets and narrow gateways, so obscured are they by shops and houses and jealous city walls. But the Cathedral on the Wiltshire plain is as English as the gentle Avon and the broad green lawns that encompass it, and as open to the gaze as the sky pierced by the Cathedral's spire. It is dominating but not arrogant, imposing without flamboyance, as lovely in the midsummer sun as when mysteriously swathed in mist, as integral a part of the landscape as the distant escarpments from which it may be seen. Perhaps, indeed, there was a further reason for Richard le Poore's choice of the Avon meadows as a site for his labours. He may well have realized that he would discover no finer setting if he ranged over the whole of Wiltshire, for on this edge of his estates the Cathedral would be visible from all directions and be equally attractive from all.

To most visitors, no doubt, the eastern approach from the London road is the most familiar one. But from the west there is the road between the lonely hills of Cranborne Chase and the winding line of the chalk downs. There is the track that climbs those heights to reward the hardy walker with magnificent views of the country to the north and Salisbury's spire to the south. All round, in quiet valleys sheltered by woods, are hamlets whose names seem to hold the essence of a bygone England. Teffont Evias, with its sixteenth-century manor house and beautiful church, or Teffont Magna, with the quarries the Romans worked and from which came much of the stone used in Salisbury Cathedral. Near by is Bemerton, where George Herbert was rector and where he is buried under the simple inscription, " G.H., 1633." And Hindon, with its dreaming houses and tree-shaded streets, which refused to return Disraeli to Parliament and which still reminds one of its vanished state.

Wilton's streets today are a poor reminder that here Egbert made good his claim to be overlord of England, that here, too, Alfred the Great defeated the Vikings, and Sweyn burnt and slew. As the ancient capital of the county, it was surveyed by Richard le Poore and wisely rejected as a site for his cathedral. It was in Wilton House, home of the Earls of Pembroke and Montgomery, that Ben Jonson and Spencer were honoured guests, that Shakespeare came to play in *As You Like It*, and that Elizabeth herself flirted with Philip Sidney. You may invoke the past also in Wardour Castle, with its paintings by Rembrandt and Velasquez, Holbein and Vandyke ; and in the ruins of an older castle besieged by Royalists and Roundheads in turn. And for the earliest of relics there are the prehistoric remains of Hanging Langford Camp, Churchend Ring and Bilbury Ring.

As for the immediate approaches to the Cathedral, the visitor is sometimes advised to enter the close by this gateway or that. The implication conveyed is false. It is a slur on a masterpiece of design. One might as well suggest that a Bach cantata, instinct with religious feeling, should be played only on the feast days of the Church. Salisbury, a stone monument of spiritual beauty, does not have to be approached from any particular direction. In its setting, it is probably the most inspiring of all cathedrals. If you come to it by the lovely St. Anne's Gate, the north front slowly and graciously unfolds itself. You may see it suddenly and impressively from the north-west, or appreciate its classic symmetry from the path to the bishop's palace in the south. You may step from your car in the parking place to an instant view of the west front. You can admire the incomparable spire through ancient trees and, if you are among the privileged, be introduced to its grey splendour from the dappled gardens of the clergy's houses. There is no best way to the Cathedral. There is a choice of ways, and all are fine.

Curiously, there have been visitors who were at first disappointed. One was the American historian, Motley, author of *The Rise of the Dutch Republic*, who put his first impressions into a lengthy letter :

" This was the first specimen of English Gothic I was to see, and as I walked thither my head was full of the Continental Gothic, which as yet was all I knew. I thought of the cathedrals of Cologne, of Vienna, of Rouen, of strange unfinished, unfinishable buildings, built according to no plan, or rather according to a dozen different ones, and rising helter-skelter from the midst of a multitude of old, sharp-gabled, red-tiled, ten-storey houses, all looking as if built in the time of the Crusaders. The idea of a Gothic cathedral was associated in my mind with hundreds of tumble-down hovels, booths and shops, mixed grotesquely here and there with a magnificent palace of half a dozen centuries . . . so that on the whole, when I came to look on Salisbury Cathedral, I was most ridiculously half-disappointed. . . .

" Influenced by the associations I have mentioned, I thought the whole scene at first too tidy, too notable, too house-wifish ; but, as I said before, this was only my own dulness ; on second thoughts I acknowledged to myself that filth and poverty and ugliness were not necessarily concomitants of a cathedral, and I confessed that I had rarely seen a more lovely picture than this same church presents. The scene is so softly and sweetly English. The stately and graceful Cathedral with its green and smooth-shaven lawn in front, the surrounding elm-trees in their magnificently massive foliage ; the tidy cottages half covered with honeysuckles and rose-bushes, the hawthorn hedges, and the green meadows with their sleek cattle (to say nothing of the macadamised turnpike and the new hotel), altogether make up a scene purely and exclusively English, and perhaps, after all as pleasing a one as you can find anywhere."

In this century, fortunately, no one rhapsodizes over hovels and filth. In this century, unfortunately, a smooth-shaven lawn surrounded by ancient elms is more Old English than English. To enter the cloisters or even the close of Salisbury is to step back into a vanished world. The cliche is unavoidable, for the plainest truths can be told only in truisms, and the word that comes first to the mind in a pilgrimage to Salisbury is " repose ".

Take the way used by most tourists, for example. They, and we, pass from the High Street through an arched gateway and in an instant the noise and petrol fumes recede and traffic lights are forgotten. The roadway is narrow, the pavement but a paved path, the little shops and houses suggest centuries of uneventful life, and the stretch of grass seen through the trees at the end of the alley might be a village green but for the glimpse of rich Gothic turrets. Then the spire comes in sight, the loftiest you can find in England. As the road widens to sweep round the close, the view suddenly broadens to range along the vast length and shapeliness of the Cathedral, which seems to rest in the wide expanse of parkland rather than to be built upon it. " A fair exterior is a silent recommendation." It is not the stateliness of the building, not its sanctity and great age, that gives one the impression of peace undisturbed even by the bombers which often fly overhead. It is the strange quality definable only by the word "repose". And this feeling of other-worldliness, of a condition of quiet and spaciousness, is deepened by the calm old houses set around the close, with doors through which one sees packed beds of sweet williams and scented stocks, marigolds and canterbury bells, and all the other simple things that should be found in English gardens.

Surely such peace is timeless ? You cannot believe that it has ever been broken. The history books must be mistaken. Historians are notoriously imaginative fellows who will stretch a fact to fill a page. But the Cathedral's own registers are above reproach. Their brief entries bring curious scenes before the reader's eyes. Here is the belfry that used to stand in the close, with its sexton selling beer to all who will buy, though at one time he is forbidden to trade for six weeks because of his impudence to the chapter.

In the belfry itself, and in the close at night, there is even more unseemly behaviour : many a woman of the town is castigated by name in the registers. As for the young vicars-general, half priests and half servants to the canons, their misdoings do not much alter throughout the centuries. They insult the close porter and make the paths unsafe by their archery and strings of dogs. They reel home at night from the taverns or, worse, steal out to assignations with the wives of decent citizens. The clatter of their clogs accompanies Divine Service in the Cathedral, and, worse again, they interrupt it by horse-play with the choristers and by brawls among themselves. Here is John Ferrant, celebrated musician of Tudor times, who tries to murder the dean, a relative of his wife ; you may read the dean's own evidence. Here is that froward Dulcibella, who has taken possession of the choristers' houses and defies the King, archbishop, three bishops and John Donne himself to move her ; so, possession being a sound point in law, the case must drag on in Chancery.

Memories of the plague stir again. The court moves to Salisbury to escape the fœtid menace of London. But in 1627 the plague creeps near the Cathedral. The clergy barricade themselves into the close, erecting platforms inside the walls so that they can climb up to receive food from the mayor and the few citizens who have not fled the city. Then they, too, escape across the plains, and for nearly a year the Cathedral is deserted. For contrast there is the close in the eighteenth century, when it becomes a minor Bath. The School of the Canons is patronized by the county's gentry, dancing masters vie with each other in organizing " elegant " balls, " academies for young ladies " spring up, concerts and plays and receptions fill the nights with decorous gaiety, and occasionally there is a highwayman to provide a subject for social chatter.

Time and again, through the ages, there is recorded the scandalous impropriety of choirmasters and other minor functionaries. Sometimes there is even conflict between the bishop and the dean. Since fact can be so incredible, perhaps the fiction of *Barchester Towers* is no stranger. It was in the close of Salisbury, you remember, that the arch-deacon paced up and down with Mr. Harding and with " war, war, internecine war " in his heart against the bishop. Perhaps even Dickens was a fair reporter in making Tom Pinch describe Salisbury as " a very desperate sort of place ; an exceedingly wild and dissipated city ".

But all that is over, and when you look at the Cathedral today it is all forgotten. Properly so, for Salisbury is not a cathedral which places its chief interest in its history. What matters most is its architecture. The layout is simple and regular. A schoolboy knowing nothing of architectural terms would describe it as being shaped like a crucifix with an additional arm, and the schoolboy would be right. It is as simple in effect ; the most untechnical of visitors must surely notice how few are the buttresses except where the tower springs from the crossing of nave and transepts. The simplicity and symmetry speak of sureness. Although the Gothic period was one of eager and ingenious experiment, the men who began this Cathedral knew what they were about and had no need to improvize. Certainly the addition of tower and spire was proof that the walls they set on soft valley soil were well built.

The sequence of events can be briefly stated. The Cathedral was begun in the year 1220 at the eastern end. The Lady Chapel was finished in 1225, and the main structure in 1258. The tower and spire were added between the years 1330 and 1350. These later builders were as ambitious as Bishop le Poore. Their spire was to be the tallest in the land ; it was to rise 404 feet above the lawn, and it was to be built without alteration to the cathedral's foundations.

This enterprise aroused the jealous contempt of later architects. Indeed, books written in our own time have described it as rash, lunatic, and so forth. Was it so ? The tower and spire still stand. A hundred years after their erection, double-arched buttresses were built across the tower arches to stiffen the slender piers. Sir Christopher Wren clamped some iron bands round the base of the tower when a subsidence threatened to split the masonry. In 1898 the tower was " restored " by Blomfield. In 1921 some of the stonework in the spire was found to have been cracked by a rusted iron clamp, which was then replaced by gunmetal. That is all that has had to be done to the original work of the early " foolhardy " builders. Inside the Cathedral, you may be shown certain marks by which any movement of the great tower can be measured. Despite all the stress and strain of our times, there has been no appreciable deviation for a hundred years. None is anticipated by the experts for a period quite as long. Yet the central towers of Winchester and Lincoln, Peterborough, Ely and Ripon all collapsed, the spire of Norwich blew down, a considerable part of St. Albans caved in. Perhaps the spire of Salisbury owes its permanence as much to wood as to stone, for it is still braced inside by the original timber scaffolding. High up inside it, too, is another feature unknown to most visitors. This is a primitive wooden wheel, which was used for hauling up the blocks of stone as the building proceeded. The interior of the spire is seldom visited. The ascent is narrow and involves much unlocking of doors. Indeed, some of the sacristans have never made the climb, and even the fire-guards during the war were not allowed higher than the clock room.

The builders of the spire achieved more than permanence, more than the tallest of English steeples. They made beauty. The spire crowns and completes the Cathedral's design, and to tower and spire the gaze irresistibly returns. They are neither too richly decorated nor too severe ; they match perfectly with the mighty building below. This is in itself remarkable, for though the main building is of the Early English style, the tower and spire are unquestionably Decorated.

The English are stubbornly inept at languages. Perhaps we are equally slow in mastering the terms in architecture. All of us have read, time and again, of the chief points of difference between the various architectural styles. Dutifully we have noted that the Normans preferred round arches, small round-headed windows and wide flat buttresses with large coarse mouldings and ornaments. The Transitional, we impressed upon our lethargic minds, was mainly a mixture of pointed arches and round ; whereas the Early English style was distinguished by tall narrow windows usually arranged in groups, piers often notable for their slender detached shafts, elaborate and undercut mouldings and beautifully carved capitals. Then, we repeated to ourselves, came the

Early Decorated vogue for wide windows divided by mullions, the Later Decorated with its increased richness generally, but more shallow and less effective mouldings—and so to the Perpendicular.

At last, we have declared, we are masters of those simple terms ; we shall not forget them. Within a week, a month at most, we are as doubtful as we were before. Fortunately, at Salisbury such forgetfulness is not a bar to appreciation ; quatrefoils and spandrels, piscina and tympanum need not roll off the tongue for the eye to be rewarded. Even he who is indifferent both to art and architecture may be impressed by such plainer facts as that the total length of the Cathedral is 473 feet, and that the nave alone is 229 feet six inches long and 84 feet high.

One thing more must be said. The symmetry, the uniformity, of Salisbury do not result in monotony. The long lines of the walls are broken by the transepts and yet preserve the continuity of design. Within, the mellow patina of stone is ribbed and barred by darker marble, severity is offset by flowing outlines, sombre grey is shot with gold and purple. When Richard le Poore drew up his plans, the Old English style was dominant. By the time the masons finished their labours, the Decorated was unfolding. Therefore, as the building progressed it was subtly moulded by changing influences, and there are also two superb examples of the later Perpendicular style. Thus, though this Cathedral of St. Mary the Virgin is the paramount achievement of one period, it reflects other styles as well.

The richness of the admired west front provides an example of this blend of styles. Architecturally, it is only a screen. Artistically, it is the most lavishly decorated part of the exterior. Its opulent central arch is the main entrance to the Cathedral, and there is a smaller arch on either side. The eleven openings above the arches were denuded of their medieval figures by the destructive zeal of the Puritans (" what the Puritans gave to the world was not thought, but action ") and these saints, virgins and martyrs were not replaced until the middle of the last century. Resting on this arcade is a trinity of the Early English windows with pointed heads which the textbooks describe as " lancets ". From the close they are leaden in appearance, but within they are afire with colour. As a whole, this great west front may be thought to suffer from a certain lack of balance between its features—between wings and turrets, the high expanse of glass and the blind, glassless lancets—but the opulence gives a variation to the simplicity notable in the other sides of the building.

It would be difficult now to suggest an addition to the Cathedral. Salisbury is not one of those unfinished, unfinishable piles of which Motley wrote. It is complete and coherent, and we may surmise that one of the reasons for this was the great wealth of the builders. Others were not so fortunate. We enter Cologne Cathedral and are informed that the present building was begun in the fourteenth century. We go on and find later dates inscribed in the stone. We go on indeed until we are surprised by a reminder of the period that we in England would call Victorian, a period when a little more money became available—and still we feel that the vast building is not complete. The main work at Salisbury was, however, done within forty years. It is true that labour was then cheap. The masons are said to have been paid a penny farthing an hour, a rate commemorated in the name of one of Salisbury's streets. None the less, the cost without the west front, the tower and spire, amounted to the modern equivalent of half a million pounds. And though the Cathedral must now appeal for funds, and its repair in 1938 was largely due to the munificence of the Pilgrims Trust, it was for long very wealthy. Indeed, the diary of old John Cooper reported succinctly in the year 1764: "The Revenues of the Cathedral are computed at about £400,000 per annum."

Its beauty of design, its wonderful setting, its grace and peace, explain why the greatest of landscape painters came to paint Salisbury Cathedral time and again. Though no building may be proof against critical analysis, here is a tall finger pointing to Perfection. As a notice in the nave says proudly: "The building composes perfectly from whatever view point."

To be sure, the composition is peculiarly suitable for the broad plains of Wiltshire. Were it set in London, or on the crags of Durham, or in so huddled a medieval city as Bruges, it would be done less than justice. It needs space for its appreciation, and its spreading close affords the proper extent of spaciousness. Its situation was not a matter of luck, but of judgment. The artistic perception of Richard le Poore and his fellows, living at a time when what we may call the " English idea " was being formulated, was responsible for the coherence of the Cathedral and the perfection of its environs. This point deserves emphasis, for it explains why the composition of our picture has never been criticized even by

> The long-neck'd geese of the world that are ever hissing dispraise
> Because their natures are little.

II

A Noble Nave

THE cool greyness of the north porch is a shrewd introduction to Salisbury's interior. It promises dignity and quietude rather than richness. The designer knew that art needs no fanfares and that the finest vistas are those which take the eye by surprise, as when a walker comes through the trees on a hillside to a sudden unfolding of the valley below. Almost instinctively, the visitor passing through the porch turns towards the great west window and so sees at once the perfection of Early English art.

Loveliness of design is allied to beauty of material ; power combines with delicacy. In these triple lancet windows—the centre one immensely high, the other two of identical proportions—is most of the stained glass that the bishops saved from the despoilers in the days of the Reformation. It dates from the thirteenth to the fifteenth centuries. The earliest examples were no doubt painted especially for the Cathedral, the later ones bear evidence of Flemish craftsmanship. Though there is uncertainty about the subjects depicted, that is a matter for scholars and clerics. The certainty is that in this glowing triplet of glass the beauty of colour is matched by the perfection of line. The windows rest on three bays of stone, nobly proportioned, and these in turn are set on a splendid arcade pierced by the double doors of the west entrance. The detail is in harmony with the design ; the whole composition is of matchless architecture.

To turn away from this excellence is to see a greater vision. The whole length of the Cathedral is revealed at a glance. No organ pipes or massive screen obstruct the gaze. The eye is led from the brightly lit nave to the dimness of the choir and the mystery of the high altar, to the ruby and violet richness of the glass in the Lady Chapel. The lines of roof and bays, the broad arches and the slender shafts of marble—these, no less than the spire, give Salisbury an exceptional place among the achievements of ecclesiastical art. It has been said that, after a while, the effect of spacious dignity hardens into a cold severity. That, however, is a personal matter, dependent on temperament and taste. Should one be lulled into worship ? Is there no place in architecture for simplicity of line ? Does grandeur consist of weighty decoration ? If not, then this Cathedral is the richer for dispensing with pomp, and the surge of admiration at the first revelation of its outline is not lessened by appraisal of its parts.

There are deep bays along the nave from the west window to the transepts on each side of the choir. Their arches have often been described as perfect. Neither narrow nor too broad, they have the simple grace of the Early English period, before the second stage of Gothic brought an abundance of ornament. So, too, with the piers between them. Because four light shafts are set around each heavy shaft, the effect is a combination of strength and elegance.   Above this lofty arcade of arch and pier is the triforium, a second line of bays unusual in design.   The arches are rounder than most which date from the same period, so that they contrast agreeably with the pointed arches below, and their massiveness is increased by the piers which support them.   Short without being clumsy, each pier consists of a core surrounded by no fewer than eighteen shafts of Purbeck marble.   Each fluted arch leads the eye to two smaller arches of similar shape, and these divide into another pair separated by a single shaft, so that the harmony of geometrical patterns provides a majestic foundation for the delicate lancets above and the sweeping curves of the vaulted roof.

This harmony is apparent throughout.   Polished marble, ranging in colour from brown to black, was deliberately chosen for the myriad shafts of the triforium arches ; it was chosen again for the slender shafts of the piers in the nave itself ; it even glistens from the ribs of the roof.   The architect used as much as would suit his purpose and no more.   He took care that Salisbury should be something more than a cathedral of marble. As if to meet the criticism that Purbeck stone is as cool to the eye as to the touch, he softened it by flowing curves.   And against the vast length and height he made the aisles on either side of the nave so much lower as to convey a feeling of intimacy despite the beautiful lancets which light their bays.

The artist who designed this grandeur was engineer as well as architect.   He was determined to build his Cathedral on soft ground.   The result might well have been an ecclesiastical Tower of London, broad, immense and squat ; instead he achieved a gracefulness that seems to spring from inspiration rather than from mathematical calculations, yet which is as strong and enduring as any deep-walled castle.   The means by which he gained his ends included a peculiar feature of the construction of the nave.   The main piers do not rise from the pavement but are set on broad low tables of stone which afford a firmer grip on the spongy soil beneath.

It is along these shallow platforms that the sculptured tombs and memorials are ranged. A murderer lies here with men who slew or were slain on the battlefield, prelates rest with earls who moulded history, a Lord Chancellor's memorial is close to that of an oculist. One small slab, between the north entrance and the west window, was for generations believed to be the tomb of a boy bishop.   It bears an episcopal figure of the kind to be seen in Winchester Cathedral : nameless, without date, obviously associated with some cleric of rank, a puzzling effigy in miniature.   What more natural than to cite it as a relic of one of the strangest chapters in Church annals ?

There seems no doubt that the custom of the boy bishop came to England early in the thirteenth century.   The remains of St. Nicholas had recently been removed from Myra to Bari, and he had become the most popular of saints and the patron of all schoolboys.   So pious that he is said to have fasted two days a week while still in the cradle, he earned in later life not only the reverence but also the gratitude of the young.   An innkeeper had lain in wait for three boys as they went home from school, had murdered them and cut up their bodies for food.   St. Nicholas raised them to life again.   To celebrate the miracle, there was dancing, singing and feasting on Innocents' Day, and in some obscure way the festival inspired the solemn ritual of the boy bishop.

He was a bishop for a day. Dressed in the gorgeous vestments of a prince of the Church, he received every mark of authority and respect. His hood was of scarlet lined with silk. Birds of gold ornamented his vesture. There were rings of rubies and silver on his fingers, and his mitre was " well garnished with perle and precious stones, with nowches of silver and gilt before and behind ". In silken robes, with copes and burning tapers, canons of his own age escorted him on the eve of Innocents' Day to the Cathedral, where he conducted a special service. From that hour until the great procession at the close of the following day, no ordained priest dare approach the altar. Meanwhile, there was merrymaking in the town. Ducks and chickens, woodcocks and larks, veal and the tenderest of lamb, pears and honey and adult quantities of ale—such was the fare for the young on Innocents' Day. Salisbury was evidently the chief centre of the festival ; there still survive twenty-one names of lads whose crook was borne with pomp into the Cathedral.

But what if the boy bishop should die during his brief tenure of office ? Surely he would be accorded the privilege of his temporary rank and be buried in the great church he ruled at the time of his death ? It was this reasoning that prompted Canon Gregory, in the seventeenth century, to assume that Salisbury's miniature tomb must commemorate so uncommon an event. There was a serious flaw in his argument. The tomb is of a size more suited to an infant of fourteen months than a lad of fourteen years. Antiquarians now agree that the slab probably covers the heart of a bishop whose body was buried elsewhere, and this view leads to another theory. Though Richard le Poore is known to have been interred in a nunnery, his heart may have been enshrined in the Cathedral that had first taken shape in his mind and which is his abiding memorial. No one will ever know. A question mark in sculptured stone, a perpetual challenge to the scholars, the slab keeps its secret.

There are other perplexities in the nave. This tomb and that have had their inscriptions blurred by the careless brush of time ; we can only speculate on the fragments of forgotten history they represent.   But there are reminders enough of the turbulent past still known to us : figures in chain mail, sword at hand and shield upraised, as if ready to start up from the pitted stone and shining alabaster.   William Longespée, half-brother of King John, natural son of Henry II and an unknown mother who may have been the " fair Rosamund ", lies next to a bishop of the thirteenth century. On the shield of this Earl of Salisbury are six golden lions to proclaim his membership of the royal houses of England and Anjou. The pose has the watchfulness of the warrior. There is sufficient colour left on the effigy to show that once the tomb had a regal magnificence.

Longespée had earned much honour in his own right. It was he who gained for England her first great naval victory. Philip of France had assembled a fleet for the invasion of these shores. But—not for the last time in our history—he thought the invasion might wait until he had vanquished a Continental enemy. Leaving the fleet poorly guarded outside the harbour of Damme, he deployed his army to besiege Ghent. Longespée saw the opportunity. Sweeping across the Channel, he first captured some three hundred vessels laden with arms and provisions and sent them under escort to

England. Next, he burned a hundred more ranged along the shore. On the following day, he drove through the remnants in the harbour like a battering ram and attacked the town. The strong forces Philip hurried to the rescue arrived too late ; England had been saved from invasion. The French revenge in the following year, when Longespée was knocked off his horse by the Bishop of Beauvais' mace and taken prisoner, was a petty incident compared with that tremendous triumph.

He might be reproached for having supported his evil half-brother, but in those days family honour was a matter more of loyalty to blood than a discriminating morality. The time came when he put country before family. He counselled John to yield to the barons, and the adoption of Magna Carta was in part due to his sense of duty. That is perhaps the highest tribute that could be paid him and the one he would most have desired.

His rough temper and dashing temperament made him incapable of cool statesmanship, though they were assets in the military tactics of his time. He so despaired of John's cause that he surrendered to Louis, but after John's death he turned against the French and his sword flashed again on behalf of the youthful Henry III when he led one of the royal armies at the battle of Lincoln. At fifty he was still hot-blooded. He joined the expedition to Gascony and, having successfully defended Guienne against Louis in 1225, set sail for home. Storms blew his ship far into the Atlantic. Suddenly, it is said, a beautiful figure was seen at the masthead, brightly illumined. Longespée had no doubt that it was the Blessed Virgin come to succour the ship's company, " for from the day of his knighthood he had provided a light to burn before the Virgin's altar ". Soon the ship was driven on to the island of Re, where Longespée found shelter in the abbey owned by a supporter of Louis. Despite his incognito he was recognized by two servants who warned him of his danger. Rewarding them well, he set sail again for Cornwall and, after a rough voyage lasting nearly three months, struggled back to safety. But his over-taxed strength had begun to fail and, brought back to his castle at Salisbury, he knew his end was near.

It was then that he showed the religious humility which had distinguished his soldier-brother, Richard Coeur de Lion. He sent for Bishop le Poore, painfully dragged himself from bed and threw himself on the floor with a rope around his throat, crying that he had been a traitor to God and begging forgiveness. The bishop must surely have been moved to compassion, for by the standards of the period Longespée had been kindly and pious, a credit to the House of Plantagenet. He died on March 7, 1226, and his body was borne in torchlit procession from castle to Cathedral through a flurry of wind and rain. His tomb was inscribed with the words "*Flos Comitum*"—Flower of Earls.

The Flower of Earls. An admirably brief epitaph ! But if your taste runs to the prolix, if you would note how times have changed the manners of obsequies, look at the pile of marble by the west window. It is surmounted by a statue of Hibernia, wrought by Rysbrack. Hibernia weeps, with handkerchief to eye. Her arm rests on a funeral urn, and in the course of the lengthy inscription below one reads not only of a lawyer's virtues but of a leisurely government which should prompt a wistful sigh from the statesmen of today :

" He presided in six Seſsions of Parliament as Speaker of the Houſe of Lords of *Ireland*, where there is a Seſsion, but once in two years.

" In April 1739. He ſat as Lord High Steward of *Ireland* on the trial of the Lord Barry of *Santry*, being the first Lord High Steward that ever was appointed in that Kingdom.

" In September 1739. He resigned his *Offices* at his own Requeſt, on account of an ill State of Health, contracted by too intent and too long application to the great Variety of Busineſs He had been engaged in.

" He was a Member of the Established Church, a strenuous Aſsertor of Lawfull Liberty, a zealous Promoter of Justice, a dutifull Subject, and a kind Relation."

In our times, brevity has found favour again ; witness the inscription by the side of the north entrance. Commemorating the death on the Somme, at the age of nineteen, of Edward Wyndham Tennant, it says simply : " When things were at their worst he would go up and down in the trenches cheering the men, when danger was greatest his smile was loveliest."

You may feel that so poignant a tribute deserves inclusion in an anthology of epitaphs. It might gain greater lustre by being set against the doggerel, the arch allusions, the pomposities and feeble jests culled from memorials in green churchyards and ancient abbeys. Salisbury has its share of quaint inscriptions, but none in obviously bad taste. Here and there the quaintness is flowery, witness the carven eulogy of the " trulie vertuous and religious " Elihonour Sadler, who appears to have been a paragon of all the conventional attributes of goodness. Fortunately, the prolixity of praise is too ingenuous to be disagreeable.

Here and there in the nave are the sarcophagi of unknown clerics. One of them is among the earliest tombs in England ; in sonorous Latin and stately periods it eulogizes the prelate for his descent from dukes and princes, his protection of the weak and his mercy to the wretched, his fearless opposition to tyrants and his scourging of the mighty. " Today men mourn at Salisberie because now is dead that sword of justice, the father of the church." But men do not mourn for ever, and even the name of this prince of the church has become only a supposition. Near by are names that revive the very atmosphere of bygone centuries—Roger the Justiciar, born in 1107, builder of Old Sarum's cathedral ; Jocelyn de Bohun ; Bishop Herman, and Walter de la Wyle.

The shrine of St. Osmund, across the nave from the north doorway, has three apertures on either side into which sick people used to thrust their arms in the hope of a cure. Then, by one of the ironies of time, it came to be reckoned as the tomb of a murderer. No ordinary murderer, to be sure. Charles Stourton was a peer of England. His family derived their name from the Stour at Stourhead, and the six apertures of the shrine were believed to signify the six sources of the river—so soon had memories waned of Salisbury's saint. Lord Stourton was an example of the bluff, cruel, impetuous barons of the Middle Ages, but even then there were some crimes that stirred the drowsy conscience of Justice. He instigated the murder of two men named Hartgill, father and son. The murders were carried out by his retainers in barbarous fashion. Tongues wagged, the reluctant law was invoked, and Lord Stourton was hanged with a silken halter in Salisbury market place. A wire noose, representing that aristocratic rope, is said to have been suspended above the tomb as a reminder of the penalty of wrongdoing.

Some people, maybe, would have placed it round the neck of James Wyatt. When the Romantic Movement was learning to walk, and there was a growing desire to " restore " ancient abbeys and cathedrals, Wyatt was the most active of human restoratives. Perhaps that is a euphemism. He has been described as a Prussian drill sergeant and an infamous vandal ; his work on the Cathedrals of Salisbury and Lichfield earned him the epithet of " The Destroyer." One cannot help suspecting that some of the other terms applied to him were due more to a desire to create an effect than to ventilate indignation. To be fair, it should be admitted that " the infamous Wyatt " was not without ability.

Born in 1746, son of a versatile farmer and builder who was also an architect and a timber merchant, he gained the patronage of Lord Bagot, ambassador to the Pope. Bagot took him to Rome, where he learned to design the mansions in the Graeco-Italian style with which he studded the English countryside. Their shapes were comely, their comfort pleasant, their decoration charming, and soon Wyatt became an adjunct to the fashionable life. He was given commissions by the House of Lords and by George III at Windsor Castle. The Duke of Devonshire and Lord Bridgewater were among his clients. He was elected a Royal Academician and appointed surveyor of Westminster Abbey, in which he came to be buried. He had a genuine appreciation of Gothic art and was largely responsible for the revival of interest in Gothic buildings. It would be easy to sneer at him and to charge him with having inspired the neo-Gothic movement which culminated in such once-admired works as the St. Pancras Hotel and the Albert Memorial. The truth is that without Wyatt and his fellow Romantics many an ancient splendour would by now be in ruins. Unfortunately, as a " restorer " and retoucher he had more enthusiasm than discretion. At Durham he scraped inches of stone off the piers and at Salisbury he juggled with stone monuments.

Originally, the tombs in the nave were placed irregularly. This seeming carelessness may well have made a pleasing contrast with the severity of the Cathedral's lines. Wyatt changed all that. He marshalled the tombs into two straight rows, and in his haste he scattered the bones of the dead, muddled the historical sequence of the memorials, and even lost a whole tomb. He did more. He destroyed some of the finest relics of Old English masonry. Probably this recital of his achievements at Salisbury is his strongest condemnation. Again, however, justice demands the admission that he was not the only despoiler, as one can see in the tomb that holds the remains of Walter, Lord Hungerford and his wife, Catherine Peverell.

Hungerford added a score of men-at-arms and threescore archers to the forces of Henry V in the invasion of France. Though it was a meagre contribution to a pitiably small army, its leader inspired one of the most resounding passages in English literature. For Hungerford was apprehensive when faced with danger but courageous when in the thick of it. In our own days such behaviour has been hailed as proof of true heroism. But when Hungerford surveyed the dense legions of the French and muttered to his royal comrade that it would be well if there were ten thousand Englishmen more in the field, Henry was contemptuous. So, of course, was Shakespeare unfair in ascribing Hungerford's remark to the Earl of Westmoreland :

KING HENRY: What's he that wishes so ?
My cousin Westmoreland ? No, my fair cousin :
If we are mark'd to die, we are enow
To do our country loss ; and if to live,
The fewer men, the greater share of honour . . .
God's peace ! I would not lose so great an honour
As one man more, methinks, would share from me,
For the best hope I have. O ! do not wish one man more :
Rather proclaim it, Westmoreland, through my host,
That he which hath no stomach to this fight,
Let him depart ; his passport shall be made,
And crowns for convoy put into his purse :
We would not die in that man's company
That fears his fellowship to die with us . . .

and so to the shattering rebuke :

And gentlemen in England now a-bed
Shall think themselves accurs'd they were not here,
And hold their manhoods cheap whiles any speaks
That fought with us upon Saint Crispin's day.

Clearly, Lord Hungerford's remark did not lose him royal favour for long. He was Steward of the Household to Henry V's successor, and Treasurer of England from 1426 to 1431. He built chantries at Chippenham and Heytesham, presented estates to the Royal Chapel at Westminster, and made bequests to the cathedrals of Salisbury and Bath. His munificence did not exclude the laity : houses for the aged poor and schoolmasters emerged from his coffers. His honours and his piety, however, meant little to a later peer. In 1778, Lord Radnor tore down the magnificent Hungerford Chantry, which once enclosed the tomb in the nave, and dragged it into the choir for conversion into a family pew.

This sacrilege would have been understandable (though not to be excused) had it been directed against the Hungerford who was an intimate of Henry VIII. His stepmother had strangled her first husband in Farleigh Castle so that she might become Lady Hungerford. When widowed again four years later, she was charged with the crime and hanged at Tyburn with one of her menservants. Young Walter Hungerford was nineteen at the time, but he was quickly consoled by being posted as one of the King's squires. His own domestic life was not without incident, for he charged his second wife with trying to poison him, imprisoned his third wife in Farleigh Castle and attempted to kill her. Then he bigamously " married " a fourth time, and his career was ended at the age of thirty-seven by the executioner's axe on Tower Hill. But that was in 1540 and he was not related to the Hungerford who had fought with Henry V a century or so earlier. The vandalistic Radnor could hardly have confused the two.

Confusion could be forgiven in one instance. There is another Hungerford tomb in the nave next to the shrine of St. Osmund. This is the tomb of Robert, Lord Hungerford, who fought in the wars against France and died in 1459 after the triumph of Agincourt had been as wantonly frittered away. The tomb is interesting chiefly because it is composed of fragments from the ruins of the Hungerford Chapel, which once stood at the other end of the Cathedral, and for the superb effigy which shows the armour of the fifteenth century. Lord Hungerford's sculptured hands lie across his breast, heavenly winged figures watch by his head, his feet rest upon a hound—and hacked into the impressive figure are the initials of louts who presumably hoped to win a vicarious immortality.

There are relics of other men who, like Henry V, were " fram'd of the firm truth of valour". William Longespee the Younger may not have been so doughty a figure in life as his father who rests on the other side of the nave, but he was surely as gallant and unselfish. It might have been better for him if he had been as quick of temper. Here in this effigy is the thin face of a cultured man, with keen eyes and sensitive lips ; chin and forehead are banded with chain mail ; the body is slim and as alert as the hand that grasps the sword hilt. He was thirty-five when he left Court with two hundred English knights to join the Crusade led by Louis of France. Louis received him with kingly courtesy, his brother Robert with princely disdain. " Long-tailed English cowards " was the mildest of the gibes coined by the French aristocrats. Longespee suffered them for the sake of the end in view. He achieved the only military success of the campaign while the French forces lay rotted by muddled and incompetent leadership—which did not prevent the French from seizing all the plunder the English had taken.

At last Longespee's diplomacy was strained by the flow of insult. He asked Louis to preserve the alliance. The French king answered that he could not control his own nobles, at which the Englishman told him bluntly that he was a poor king and then withdrew his forces to Syria. An appeal from Louis induced him to return. Longespee succeeded in crossing the Nile and came upon the Egyptian army. Prudently he advised Robert, who advanced with a small detachment, to wait until Louis arrived with the main French forces, whereupon Robert accused him again of long-tailed cowardice. Longespee said quietly, " I shall go today where you will not dare to keep level with the tail of my horse." It was magnificent, but it was not war. The dash into the spreading ranks of the Egyptians and the destruction of so much English chivalry was suicidal ; the ensuing rout of the French army and the capture of Louis had not the merit even of a grand gesture. Probably Longespee's tomb in Salisbury is empty. Perhaps he was buried in the Church of the Holy Cross at Acre. It is not certain that his body was recovered from the bloodstained desert.

There is a Montacute close by, next to the sepulchre of Walter, Lord Hungerford. It is the Sir John who died in 1390, brother of the founder of the line of Montacute Earls of Salisbury. Here, too, confusion threatens. This is not the John Montacute who advised King Richard III to flee to Bordeaux, who counselled the arrest of the Duke of Gloucester and the Earl of Warwick, raised revolt against the newly crowned Henry VII, was threatened with death by the citizens of London as a high traitor and despoiler of sacred images, and who indeed died on the block and had his head set up on a spike at London Bridge. This John who sleeps in the peace of Salisbury is a sedate figure. But he fought at Crecy, and who would begrudge a veteran of Crecy so imposing an effigy, such rich decoration of armour ? We are therefore free to admire the highly ornamented gauntlets, the " contrivance for the easier bending of the body at the bottom of the breastplate, and of the elegant manner of twisting the hanging sword belt, pendant from the military girdle, round the upper part of the sword ", and the lion that crouches by his feet.

It is at the crossing of nave and transept that the most sumptuous memorial stands. The size of this alabaster sepulchre is not a matter of pride and pomp, for here rest the remains of a giant.   Moreover, Sir John Cheney was as heroic in deed as in stature.   In full armour, with sword or axe in gigantic hand, he must have been an intimidating antagonist ; his thighbone alone was a good four inches larger than the average man's. He did not intimidate Richard III, however, when the two clashed on Bosworth Field. Cheney had the strength of a titan, Richard the strength of desperation.   On the face of it, the odds were weighed against the tiny band clustered round Henry Tudor.   Richard's army was nearly three times as large.   Among its leaders were the gallant Howards—the Duke of Norfolk and his son—and others willing to cry, " My king, right or wrong." Willingness, lacking the fire of zest, could not communicate itself to the rank and file.

Richard's army faltered, broke, and melted like an ice pack in a tropical current.   It was Richard himself who best fought his own battle.   Warped, venomous, pitiless and evil, the last of a brave line of kings, he did not dishonour his last hour.   Though his men were throwing away arms and standards, leaving him unprotected, he charged into the knights closely ringed about the Tudor prince.   His axe swung this way and that, cutting through swords as a scythe among stubble.   Henry's standard bearer, Sir William Brandon, was brought down ; the gigantic Cheney followed him, though he was to recover and live another twenty years.   As the axe was raised against Henry himself, when in one moment more Richard would have preserved his throne, the King was borne down by the press of knights on either side and battered to death.

III

Salisbury's Treasures

WHERE the brightness of the nave is emphasized by the shadows of the choir, two arches give entrance to the transepts on either side. No one has ever given an adequate description of those arches. It may be that they are beyond the skill of any writer. If he speaks of them as engineering devices, as supports for the central piers, he leaves the reader unmoved. If he testifies that their Perpendicular form is set against the surrounding Early English style and harmonizes with it, he does them less than justice. If he seeks to describe their majestic design, their grace, the beauty of their decoration, he must string so many superlatives together as to risk being accused of hyperbole. He can do no more than to state that they are sublime, to suggest that Britain has no lovelier examples of their kind, and to trust that the memories of readers who have seen them will compensate for his own deficiencies.

To insist that here also is the Cathedral's finest view is rather like answering those absurd questions about " the world's best books" or "the greatest composer". At least it can be said with safety that this part of the interior deserves special attention. On the left, at the end of the south transept, is the twelfth-century window which many people consider even richer than the great west window; but the shrewdest visitor is he who, taking a few steps into the transept towards it, turns to look back and upwards. He turns to see lovely lancets and double-light windows in the other transept, with the lines of the narrow vaulting sweeping up from them. He sees the greater loftiness and more open roof of the crossing, and his gaze also takes in a little of the subdued tones of the choir, the richly carved stalls, the lightness of the gilded screen. He sees the pulpit that, though modern, accords perfectly with its setting. He sees curve soaring from curve to envelop other curves—and all this is framed by one of those incomparable Perpendicular arches, delicately fretted from pale stone yet powerfully battlemented, glinting from one pier with gold and silver and soft green from the miniature effigy of a saint, with the equally beautiful twin arch beyond. At such a vision the heart is uplifted as by great poetry.

How easily such a vision could have been ruined ! In some cathedrals a noble view is utterly spoiled by organ pipes, and though you may be a devotee of organ music you will admit that its apparatus is not a thing of beauty. In Salisbury, the organ is inconspicuous. It is divided into two parts, one on either side of the choir. The connecting machinery is hidden in a tunnel under the pavement, and the larger pipes and bellows enclosed within a screen. So the eye is not distracted while the ear is charmed by a particularly fine instrument.

The monuments in the transepts can hardly compete in design with the twin arches that lead to them, even though they include three by Flaxman and one by Chantrey. You will observe nevertheless that much attention is paid by visitors to the celebrated clock which now rests in the north transept after its centuries of labour. Made entirely of wrought iron, it had no dial and struck only the hours. Probably the oldest clock in the land, it dates from the year 1386 or perhaps a little earlier. In the south transept is the richly gilded chapel of St. Michael, dedicated to the dead of the first World War. In both transepts the tall lancet windows, supported by recessed lancets that occupy the whole width of the wall, give a brilliance that emphasizes the mystery of the choir.

That heart of the Cathedral was not always so religious of aspect. "The Choir of Salisbury resembles a theatre rather than a venerable Choir of a Church; it is painted white, with the panels golden, and groups and garlands of roses and other flowers intertwined round the top of the stalls; each stall hath the name of its owner in gilt letters on blue writ on it, and the episcopal throne with Bishop Ward's arms upon it would make a fine theatrical decoration, being supported by gilt pillars, and painted with flowers upon white." Such was the criticism of Defoe who, whatever his political evasions, was usually an accurate reporter. There is no indecorous gaiety in the choir today. Peer into the deepest recesses of the carving on throne and stalls and you see no relic of white or gold: the lions rampant and alligators and other figures surmounting the benches are as sedate of hue as the floor itself. Even the Bishop's throne, for all its modernity, looks no more recent than the thirteenth-century seats.

Nor is the whole scene one of unrelieved dimness. A silver crucifix gleams from its case beside a vase of flowers. There is a glow from the distant windows of the Lady Chapel and the gold of the High Altar. Above all, painted on the vault itself, are the coloured medallions which faithfully reproduce the style of medieval painting. Their originals were obliterated by a colour wash during the alterations to the Cathedral in 1790. They appear to have been the work of Italian artists brought to England by Henry III. Twenty-four of the medallions portray holy men and angels, a dozen more depict the months of the year. Against their light background they are pleasing without being arresting, just as one can say of the reredos that it is ornate but otherwise unremarkable.

Supporting the vault, dividing choir from choir aisles, are slender-shafted piers, and in design and decoration the eastern end is—no other word will apply—unique. The central arch is flanked by two narrower and taller arches, surmounted by five blank arches; above are blind arches flanking a central triplet of glazed lancets. These last, with boldly modelled figures and splendid colours, represent Moses and the brazen serpent. They were erected by the Earl of Radnor in 1781 (by way of contrition for his desecration of the Hungerford Chantry?), and they are headed by fine mouldings. The effect is attractive but strange. For a moment one has the impression of being in a Moorish temple. Two features contribute to the sense of unfamiliarity, and both are concerned with the lower arches. There is the unusual, un-English, shape of the side arches. There are the colours which adorn all three. Line on line of different and rather indeterminate hues are unexpected in such a position, yet these, too, prove that Salisbury is an architectural symphony of several tones but coherent as a whole.

In the aisles on each side of the choir are soft shafts of light and pools of deepest shadow, and memorials that are works of art and relics of extreme antiquity. Some of these last are beautiful, some are literally ghastly. There is the lovely tomb of Roger de Mortival, Bishop from 1115 to 1130. Then there are the skeleton effigies, with lipless mouths and empty caverns for eyes, with shrunken frame and bare-ribbed chests, to shock passers-by into realization of the briefness of life and the crudity of death. We may presume that these grim warnings in stone were favoured by the secular rulers as well as the spiritual teachers of the Middle Ages. Kings who sat uneasily on their thrones were never adverse from reminding their subjects that life could as easily be truncated by the headsman's axe as by bubonic plague.

Beside these cadaverous exhibits in the north choir aisle lies the body of a bishop who died preaching. Salisbury's bishops would make a remarkable portrait gallery. Some were esteemed as saints, one was battered to death by a mob, one was a scholar, the next knew no Greek but was skilful in affairs of State, another was as agile in political allegiances as the Vicar of Bray. John Jewel, most famous of the later bishops, was both saintly and practical. He had learning, kindliness, a prodigious memory and an un-flagging energy. Though his writings lacked fire, they were so closely argued and clearly expressed that they made a considerable impression among educated men on the Continent as well as in his own country. His " Apology for the Church of England " informed Europe of the need for the newly founded Anglican Church. Despite such claims on his time, he did not neglect his diocese. He built a library at Salisbury, and took poor boys into his own house to train them for the university. His body wasted with the demands made upon it, but he would not curtail his activities. In 1571 he set out on another tour of the diocese. Told he was so ill that the strain would kill him, he retorted gently, " A bishop had best die preaching ", and in truth he preached his last sermon before his visitation was finished.

Other bishops rest in the choir aisles. A finely canopied monument is probably the tomb of Walter Scammel, Bishop of Salisbury so long ago as 1284-86. There is Simon of Ghent, whose bishopric ended in 1315. The printed card before one monument says simply that it is the " Cenotaph of Richard Poore, Bishop, 1217-1229, a founder of this cathedral, 1220, died at Durham, 1237 ". Bursting with gold and scarlet from the deepest dimness of the south aisle is the large, neo-classical, Jacobean monument which in gilt letters proclaims itself as the tomb of " Richard Mompesson, Knight, and Katherine his wife ". Its richly coloured effigies are set about with urns and shields and coats of arms, a cherub's face and statuettes. Elsewhere the memorial might have been flamboyant ; here it has a sombre opulence.

The visitor is tempted to turn aside, halfway down either aisle, into a choir transept. The temptation is admirable, for though these two transepts are smaller than the main transepts, their interest is more varied. In the southern one, for example, is the immense and ancient vestment chest which looks like an enormous grand piano. The heavy lid was originally lifted by rope and windlass, and probably the chest is as old as the Cathedral itself.   Near by is an exquisite jewel of stonework, one of the most precious in England : the chantry of Bishop Giles de Bridport.   Angels bearing censers support the effigy's head.   Scenes from the prelate's life are sculptured in bas-relief on the lovely shrine that encloses the tomb.

It was a rich life.   He became Dean of Wells in 1253, and arbitrated in a dispute between the abbot and monks of Abingdon.   In 1255 he was archdeacon of Berkshire. A year later, as Bishop-elect of Salisbury, he was King Henry III's envoy to Pope Alexander IV, to meet whose demands the " clergy and people of England " were heavily taxed. His journey was not without hazard.   The French laid traps for him ; he eluded them. Returning to England, he found his new Cathedral nearly finished.   He covered its roof with lead.   The great west front dates from his time.   He saw the solemn consecration of the finished building by Archbishop Boniface of Savoy, in the presence of the King and many bishops.   A man of learning and generosity, he deserved to be immortalized by this magnificent tomb.

The decoration, in and around two arches which each envelop two openings separated by a single shaft of stone, explains the fascination this masterpiece holds for students of architecture :   it is a record of the development of the Early English style into that of the Decorated.   In this choir transept, moreover, is the threshold to relics of ancient English life and social history.   A doorway, small and modest, leads into a building that is small, two-storied and octagonal.   The walls are so thick that originally they must have guarded the Cathedral's treasure.   In a sense, they still do, for though the ground floor is now the vestry, the upper floor houses the Cathedral's muniments which are not to be seen by ordinary visitors.

Here in a glass case is a charter granted by King Stephen at Oxford in 1136.   Here, for contrast, are the legal documents of commoners :   the will of Philip Aubyn, citizen of Winchester, dated 1328 ;   the grant by John le Spicer to John Steyde of a messuage in " Brounestrete ".   The names alone in these manuscripts are proof of the imperceptible changes in the language since Salisbury was new :   Roger de Brinkewrthe, William Fresepanis, William of Heghteresburi, Nicholas of Tyngewik, John Espiciarius, Gilbert de Whichtheburi.   And the dry phrases summon up pictures of a pettifogging legalism, of lawyers in snuff-coloured gowns and priests with shaven heads, of quaint payments and sacred observances.

Consider the grant of " Robert, called of Romeseya, perpetual vicar in the greater church of Salisbury, to Robert, called of Gernemutha, likewise perpetual vicar, of a court in the close, with freedom to assign, so it be to a canon or vicar, subject to a payment of 5s. on the feast of the Purification and of 2½ lb. of wax on All Saints' *ad lumina in capella beate Virginis.*"   The date is June 6, 1290.   Turn to the grant of " John de Opere, son of Robert de Opere, to masters William de La Riuere and Richard de Nogent, clerks, of a tenement in the street leading from the canons' close to the church of St. Martin, to be held of the church of St. Mary the Virgin of Salisbury.   *Et ad maiorem hiuus rei securitatem liberaui predictis magistris Willelmo et Ricardo una cum presenti carta omnia instrumenta que penes me habui de predicto tenemento.* Witnesses : Master Ralph of York, chancellor ; sir William of Braybrock', and Stephen of Rammesburi, canons ; master William Hervy, clerk ; master William of Schyrebourn', sir John of Winchester, William of Wokyngham, William of Stok', Ralph of Stevenhache, vicars in the church aforesaid ; Roger of Stock', bailiff ; Reginald of Todeworth, mayor ; John le Stut and Philip Aubyn, coroners ; Adam Leyrenmanggere and Alan of Canygges, reeves ", and others. The date is " the Thursday before the Nativity of St. John Baptist, 1302, 30 Edw. I ".

The records also tell of disputes and grave sins. The mandate of Pope Gregory X thunders against the prior of Bernewell for the restitution of the property unlawfully taken away from the Cluniac priory of Castel Acra, in the diocese of Norway ; disobedience will be met by the pain of excommunication. A settlement is announced in the suit, heard before the prior of St. Frideswide, Oxford, and other judges delegated by the Pope, of Henry Tessun, rector of Niwenton, and the "abbat and convent" of Glastonbury, whereby the rector retains the tithes on payment of three marks yearly to the abbot and convent, and undertakes to obtain the confirmation of the bishop and chapter of Salisbury. Skip the centuries, to the October of 1634, and read the submission of certain parishioners of Beaminster, in the peculiar jurisdiction of Canterbury, who have been presented at the late visitation of Archbishop William Laud " for not bowing or using lowly reverence in the time of divine service when the blessed name of the Lord Jesus is mentioned ". They confess, these sinners against the canon, that " they did it in ignorance, for want of readinge the same yerely in the church ". They crave pardon and promise future obedience.

Edward I warns those about to visit Salisbury not to disturb the canons. Edward II acknowledges the payment of a hundred marks into his chamber by the dean and chapter as a fine for the appropriation of the church of Henneye. Henry III sends letters patent to Richard le Poore. Edward IV writes to the dean asking that his daughter Isabel shall be granted underwood for fuel from the dean's woods at Godalmynge. There are letters stamped with the Great Seal, exempting the inhabitants of the close from the authority of the stewards, marshals and other servants of the royal household. There are charters from King Stephen, Henry I and Henry II ; royal pardons from the time of Henry V to that of Edward VI, letters from Elizabeth and other monarchs. Here, from the council of Edward VI, is a confession of royal bankruptcy :

" After our hartie commendacions. Forasmoche as the Kynges Maiesties mynte of Brystowe is presently destitute of Bullion, and in that your Cathedrall Churche there is certein plate amountyng to the somme of twoo thowsande markes, consideryng the nerenes to the mynte and present necessitie it might stande the Kynges highnes in good stede. Therefore these are to desyre you to delyver the said plate uppon a byll of Robert Recordes hande to his highnes vse and we shall geve ordre that ye shall be repayed with thanckes. The shortnes of the tyme and importaunce of the matter requyreth expedicion. And therefore we eftsones pray you to satisfie our desyre in this behalfe. And thus fair you hartely well. From Westminster the Last of July, 1549.

Your louing Frendes.

E. Somersett.   W. Seynt John.
Anthony Wynkefeeld.   William Peter.

To our very good Lorde the busshopp of Salisbury and to our Louing frendes the Dean and Chapter there."

We shall meet with the all-powerful " Somersett " again.   Meanwhile, let us watch Elizabeth, iron barely concealed in her dainty glove, as she writes to the bishop, dean and chapter :

Elizabeth R.

Trusty and welbeloved we grete you well.   Wheras wee haue now at length vnderstood by our seruant Walter Raleighe Knight, Captain of our Garde, that you are growen to some agreament for the passing of a better estate at Shirburne, according to our former recommendation by the hand of our Archbushopp of Canterbury, and others of our Counsayle; wherin it hath appeared unto you, both in his opinion and in the opinion of our Bushopp of that Dyocesse, that wee did require nothing of you, that might touch any of you in Conscience, or Credytt, that were to give your assent vnto it.

To the intent that you may now (for your better satisfaction) knowe, that it was our desyre (in respect of the gentlemans services and his great charge bestowed upon his lease) to haue such an estate confirmed, we haue thought good to lett you understand that wee do thanckfully accept the same at your handes and do expect the accomplishement thereof with all convenient expedition.

And where you desyre that wee wilbe pleased to be so gratious to that Churche as to promyse not to make this a president for other sutes of lyke nature to be heaped uppon you ; we are content to lett you knowe that thoughe the extraordinary expense he hath ben at, and the danger which his Estate was subject vnto, did iustly moue vs, to seeke to procure hym that assurance, which by your Grant shall be passed to hym, yet you shall not need to mistrust that we wilbe easely drawen at any tyme, to use the aucthority of our recommendation to you, ether of this kind, or any other, to the preiudice of that Sea, whereof wee haue alwaies had, and will haue, a gratious consideration.

But where wee vnderstand that you have held hym so hard in this Composition, as you haue strayned him to the payment of lx *li* a yeare, more than he receaued, or did pay heretofore ; wee must confesse, that wee cannot but thincke but you haue proceaded herein with less respect, ether for the tyme or the matter that wee did exspect, wherof if we find you shall take any second Consideration, more in his fauour, in regard of our recommendation, wee shall make a muche better interpretation bothe of your former backwardnes, and of your present yelding, considering all the reasones, which wee haue vsed and layd before you, in the best sort of your owne profession.

Given under our Signett at the Manner of Grenewich the xxvth day of Julij in the xljth yeare of our Raigne 1599.

This mighty epistle may be more artfully expressed than the missive once sent to a bishop of Ely, and which ran—to quote from memory—as follows : " Proud Prelate,— Remember what you were before I made you what you are now.   If you do not at once comply with my design, I will unfrock you, by God. *Elizabeth.*"   Perhaps she had more respect for the Bishop of Salisbury and his chapter, but it is clear that no bishop could hope to thwart her.

IV

Romance in Brass and Stone

FROM such glimpses of other ages, it is good to take a wider view of what seems to be another world. So one should descend the steps of the ancient treasure house, return through the choir transept into the choir aisle—and pause.

Flanking the splendid gateway to the choir itself are five modern figures of saints : four on one side, St. Monica alone on the other. But the brilliance of their gold and green and purple is only the foreground of the picture ; the eye is attracted to the vaulting of the opposite transept seen over the bays of the choir. Resting on the opening arch is an immense inverted arch, designed no doubt to withstand the pressure of the mighty tower and spire. Beyond, soaring upwards, are the ribs of the roof, receding into a dimness pierced by a shaft of ruby light from a stained glass window.

The effect must vary with personal taste and mood. There are some who give no more than a casual glance, some who may unfavourably compare the heaviness of the inverted arch with similar arches elsewhere, but some also who feel here a sense of mystery and awe that the builders of great churches rightly sought to evoke. The feeling is not lessened by re-entering the choir, crossing the presbytery between the glory of the altar and the restraint of the carved stalls, and passing through to the northern choir transept that afforded so impressive a view but a moment ago.

Inset into the floor of this transept, and likely therefore to be unnoticed, is one of the finest brasses in existence. It shows a tall tower of four stages, as if the keeps of four castles had been piled on each other, with battlements and many arrow slits and lookout posts. Framed in the gateway is a simply clad warrior whose appearance would be ingenuous but for sword and shield. Above and beyond him, many times larger than the laws of perspective allow, is a mitred bishop at prayer. This is Robert de Wyville, nominated to Salisbury in the fourteenth century by Queen Philippa. He was not popular. The jealous described him as ugly and illiterate, and one episode in his career has led to the explanation that the armed gentleman in the brass was his champion. For Wyville disputed the right of William de Montacute, Earl of Salisbury, to the possession of Sherborne Castle. The Earl cunningly retorted that he would maintain his right by single combat ; the Bishop, lacking experience with the sword though skilful with the staff, accepted the challenge—and appointed a champion in his place. The great Earl, friend of the King, rode out to the combat. Then came an inglorious hitch. It was found that the Bishop's champion had, beneath his armour, girded his loins with parchment texts and his chest with written prayers. The Earl protested, the champion insisted that spiritual armour was as legitimate as temporal chain mail. The combat was deferred for the dispute to be argued, legal advice was sought, and in the end justice was done by Wyville winning the castle on payment of 2500 marks to the Earl. Still, the Bishop deserved his handsome memorial in the transept. It was he who enlarged the Cathedral cloisters. He completed the wall of the close, with stone from the old Norman cathedral in deserted Sarum. Above all, he is credited with building the spire.

Around the tablet is some of Salisbury's latest and oldest stonework. There is the fine Late Decorated trough for the washing of hands, the double aumbry for holding sacred vessels. On the western wall is an Early English screen of magnificent workmanship. Carved heads, a little defaced by age, spring from arches which are themselves well sculptured ; the slim shafts of the piers are crowned by ornate capitals. It is thought that once this screen stood by the entrance to the choir and was torn away by " the infamous Wyatt ", but the conjecture is too tentative to be added to the accusations against that well-meaning vandal.

After such digressions into the choir transepts, the tour of the choir aisles must be completed. On the southern side, by the effigy of Richard le Poore, is the Audley Chapel or chantry. Bishop Audley died in 1524, and this chantry has the delicacy of detail characteristic of the Late Perpendicular. The design is, however, so unusual that it is worth examination from both the choir aisle and the choir itself. In the aisle, the difference between the two bays of the chantry is not so apparent as the beautiful fabric of the canopy and cornice. Here is stone laboriously cut by the mason's chisel into the intricacy of old lace and seemingly as light as silk. But from the altar steps, the bays are seen to be oddly dissimilar. The one resembles the iron-barred window of a fortress, the other provokes the irreligious analogy of the tiers of boxes in a theatre. Neither artist nor cleric can be found to praise the composition while admiring the workmanship.

The sacristans are sometimes embarrassed, too, by the Hungerford Chantry on the other side of the choir. Or, rather, by the remains of the chapel so indecorously transformed into Lord Radnor's pew. The sacrilege in the nave has resulted in the chapel presenting an odd appearance to visitors in the south choir aisle : it appears to be a blank wall surmounted by tall, grim iron bars, and the effect from the choir is hardly more inspiring. " Surely the Cathedral never had its own prison ? " bewildered innocents ask. It is fair to add that the sacristans, though they must be tired of the question, still answer with tact and courtesy. At one time the chantry must have had splendour. There are notes and drawings which pay tribute to the dignity of its Late Perpendicular design, the gorgeous sculpture, the shudders inspired by the wall paintings of the Dance of Death, the majestic placing of the tomb.

There are other losses. The Beauchamp Chapel has disappeared. Not even a full account of its glories has survived ; cursory references alone suggest that it surpassed the Hungerford Chapel in beauty. We know that in it were the finely canopied tombs of Bishop Beauchamp and his parents, and Sir John Cheney's sepulchre which now stands in the nave, that the roof was of Irish oak and the masonry was the crown of late Gothic art—no more. The excellence of the fragments which survive in the Lady Chapel are the chief reasons for deploring the loss of the whole. Even the Lady Chapel, first part of the Cathedral to be completed and its easternmost end, has suffered loss. Here, where the altar now stands, was the shrine of St. Osmund, erected in or about the year 1457 after his canonization.

The design of the Lady Chapel has been the cause of controversy. It consists of four bays, and for half its length is flanked by the choir aisles, so that it has a remarkably open aspect. No one has disputed the beauty of the contoured roof, but the piers which support the roof are certainly extraordinary. One has the impression that the designer anticipated Cobden. " Sir, the thing is impossible," said a critic to that great man. " Indeed ? " said Cobden, " then the sooner we set about doing it the better." At first sight it would seem impossible that such slender shafts of Purbeck marble, no more than a few inches in diameter, could support the vault. The conception was daring. The construction was successful. But is the design satisfactory ?

One school has attacked it strongly, complaining that the piers are as ugly as scaffolding poles and look as though they might snap at any moment. To which the defenders answer that the parts of a building should fulfil their function without fussiness, and that columns do not need to be obese in order to be shapely. The lighting of the chapel has also had its detractors. The wall has a lovely triplet of stained glass ; on either side is a single graceful lancet. Some people object that these flanking lights are too independent of the centre windows to form a quintuplet, and that they are too boldly coloured to provide the focal point of the chapel's glass. Other people maintain that boldness and variation are preferable to uniformity. The colours of the chapel are arresting. The narrow shafts, of so dark a green as to appear black, stand out against the lighter green of the vault, the ribs of which are painted with white and red and green again. You may feel that the chapel as a whole matches the splendid lightness which prevails throughout most of the Cathedral ; or you may feel that it reflects more audacity than restfulness. The certainty is that it must have been an effective contrast to the Hungerford and Beauchamp chantries which once were on either side of it, and fragments from which it now contains.

Beneath the windows are niches from the Beauchamp Chapel. Their canopies are stately, their tracery delicate. The three central niches of the reredos were actually the reredos of the Beauchamp Chapel, those on either side were probably taken from demolished doorways. It may be unwise to dogmatize on such topics as religious propriety and artistic decency. Many a period has brought a vogue for ill-considered " improvements " and "renovations", and our own times have not been without the errors of destruction. But at least one imagines that today any project to rend apart ancient and jewelled chantries would be vigorously opposed.

On the left of the Lady Chapel, the north choir aisle is ended by the sepulchre of Sir Thomas and Lady Gorges an ornate and inchoate memorial typical of Jacobean extravagance, with twisted columns, symbols of the cardinal virtues and so forth, making a rather impressive whole by the sheer weight of its pretentiousness. On the other side of the Lady Chapel is the tomb, not less curious, of William Wilton, Chancellor of Salisbury from 1506 to 1523. It is a pity that a silken cord prevents close inspection, for apart from the emblems signifying Wilton's association with Henry VIII, Catherine of Aragon and other celebrities, there is inscribed a pun on his name.   Still nearer to the Lady Chapel is the towering and arresting memorial to the bearer of an illustrious name : Edward Seymour, Earl of Hertford.

It is said that Heine was shadowed all his life by a mysteriously cloaked figure. Similarly, you may find this golden tomb shadowed by the figure of a greater Seymour than he who lies here.   The ambitious, dictatorial, the incredible Thomas Seymour ! At thirty, "young and wise but of small power", he brings Anne of Cleves to London. Such a mark of royal trust is significant, yet he is not content to be a courtier.   He sees himself as a master of statecraft.   Probably it is he who engineers the downfall of the King's chief counsellor, Thomas Cromwell.

Seymour leads an army against the Scots.   Offered the keys of Edinburgh in return for a pledge of clemency, he refuses them.   Nothing less than unconditional surrender will satisfy him.   Canongate is blown up, his troops pillage the capital, he loads ships at Leith with spoil for England.   Now his influence grows rapidly.   He is Lieutenant of the kingdom during Henry's absence in France.   When Henry VIII dies, he dares to keep the news secret while he hurries to Hertford to secure possession of the new boy King Edward VI.   He dares even to use the royal " we " in the letter reporting his action. Returning with the young King to the Tower, he is rewarded with " the name and title of Protector of all the realms and domains of the King's majesty, and governor of his royal person ".   At the coronation, he is High Steward of England.   Eight days later he is appointed Treasurer of the Exchequer and Earl Marshal besides.   Another five days pass, and he is created Baron Seymour of Hache ; a few days more, and he becomes the Duke of Somerset.

Now he attains almost to regal authority ; indeed, he is the first really Protestant ruler of England.   He addresses the King of France as " brother".   He speaks of himself as " caused by Providence to rule".   Earnest for religious reform, he corresponds with Calvin and informs the bishops that henceforth they are officers of the State ; Cranmer is putty in his hands.   May he not even be able to unite England and Scotland ?   That, in truth, would be the great seal of his fame, his supreme service to his country.   He will seek to marry Edward VI to Mary of Scotland. . . . But there are mutterings against his vast power.   They swell in volume and are translated into action.   He falls sick, and in his feebleness is not able to combat the plot against him and to stave off his arrest.   He is dignified to the end.   As his head falls from the block on Tower Hill, the crowd presses forward to dip handkerchiefs in his blood.   His body is buried next to Anne Boleyn and Catherine Howard in the Tower Chapel. . . .

Edward, the son who lies here, could not match that tremendous record.   But he was no nonentity, no disappointment to the high state in which he was born.   He dared to defy the most imperious monarch in our history, and his life deserves the adjective of " romantic".   His godparents were dukes, and as a young man he was a hostage in France. Then, clandestinely, he married Catherine Grey, sister of Lady Jane.   Eventually the marriage became known.   Queen Elizabeth, furious that her permission had not been sought, sent bride and groom to the Tower. The latter was also summoned to the Star Chamber and fined £15,000. There was bitter criticism of the Queen for so extortionate a fine, and she quickly remitted £10,000. But the gesture did not imply forgiveness.

Catherine bore her two sons in the Tower, then she died. Perhaps it was her death that softened a jealous heart and won the royal clemency; for a while Edward was imprisoned in pleasant country houses. But Elizabeth erred if she thought he had been tamed. Though the woman he loved was buried, the cruel injustice they had suffered burned through his grief. Their marriage had been invalidated—so monstrously petty Elizabeth could be in her greatness—and he was resolved that the annulment should be set aside. For his presumption, he was again sent to the Tower. True, he was freed after a month or two, and later he was to be appointed Ambassador-Extraordinary to Brussels, Lord Lieutenant of Somerset and Wiltshire, and High Steward of the Revenues to Queen Anne. Though the pathos of his life could not be compensated, it is right that he and his unhappy Catherine should rest side by side in the dignified tomb that, restored by a Duke of Northumberland, assures them of immortality in name.

But Salisbury has reminders, too, of another side of the strange, enigmatic woman who sat on England's throne when Shakespeare was alive. She took a liking to a bluff, forthright, burly and unprepossessing divine named Guest (or Gheast or Geste), who had helped to settle the affairs of the newly reformed Church. He applied for the deanery of Worcester. Elizabeth thought that Worcester was too far from London. She appointed him archdeacon of Canterbury instead. Later, the Archbishop of Canterbury asked her to appoint him to the vacant see of Durham. Elizabeth thought that Durham was too far from London. Guest became the Queen's chief almoner. He was elected chancellor of the Order of the Garter. He was chosen as one of her Lent preachers. As final proof of her favour, she made him Bishop of Salisbury, in the choir of which he was buried, and his blunt features were depicted in a brass that was later moved from the choir to the north transept. Gloriana could be generous.

V

Richness and Simplicity

FAME, we know, is an unreliable guide to excellence. She keeps before us the features of a stout burgher whose only merit was that he paid Rembrandt to paint his portrait, but she has kept no record of the man who first made fire or paper. She erects statues to the memory of generals whose trumpeted victories deflected the course of history for only a year or two, yet condemns to perpetual obscurity men whose creations have endured for centuries. Therefore you will find no monument in Salisbury's streets to the memory of the bishop (probably Robert de Wykehampton) who was responsible (probably between the years 1270 and 1280) for the chapter house which is reached by going through a door in the south transept and walking halfway down the east gallery of the cloister.

Admirers of the Cathedral claim that this chapter house is the most beautiful in Britain. Even a critic might be constrained to admit that though other chapter houses may be equally stately, none surpass it. In fact, there never has been such a critic, so far as one can trace. Nor has anyone denied that the chapter house is the most perfectly symmetrical and graceful member of a cathedral famous for its symmetry and severe beauty. Its design is simple, and so can be described quite simply.

Octagonal in shape, it is fifty-eight feet in diameter and fifty-two high. As with buildings of similar purpose at Westminster and Wells, it has a central pillar from which the groining of the roof springs in gracious curves, and round the core of the pillar are eight slender shafts of Purbeck marble. The tiles on the floor are reproduced from a Norman pavement. Around seven of the eight sides runs a stone bench, with a lower ledge for clerical feet and with the merciful provision of heating pipes to mitigate the coldness of stone in winter. Serving as a back for the seating is a canopied arcade, its arches borne on Purbeck marble shafts. Above is a series of sculptured reliefs, and all this is a plinth which supports seven huge and lovely Early English windows, separated by powerful piers. Facing the entrance, the blind arcading is recessed and curtained to denote the seats of the bishop, the dean and archdeacon, while on either side of the entrance the chancellor and treasurer have their places.

With that, simplicity ends and richness begins. The contour of the windows is splendid enough to rival the Decorated style. Each arch envelops two secondary lights, each of these divides into two lancets, and the tracery of the heads is very fine. The bosses of the roof are elaborately carved. And the high reliefs above the canopy are celebrated for their boldness of execution and their vigorous sense of action. Originally they were brightly painted, but a puritanical Commission which sat in the building during the Great Rebellion was shocked by such levity and defaced them savagely. The heads thus battered have been restored, fortunately, with considerable fidelity to the originals, so that the series remains a glorious example of medieval sculpture. It presents sixty scenes. Here are Adam and Eve in the Garden, with apple and serpent; here is Noah's Ark to delight very young visitors; here, too, is a wonderful earthquake scene which startlingly foreshadows the modern manner. It will be noticed, taking them in order from the doorway, that these episodes from Old Testament history show a marked preference for the subjects offered by Genesis:

Chaos.	Rachel, Jacob and Laban.
Creation of the Firmament.	Jacob and the Angels.
Creation of the Earth.	The Angel touching Jacob's thigh.
Creation of the Sun and Moon.	Jacob meeting Esau.
Creation of Birds and Fishes.	Joseph's Dream.
Creation of Adam and Eve.	Joseph relating the Dream.
The Seventh Day.	Joseph in the Pit.
The First Marriage.	Joseph sold into Egypt.
The Temptation of Eve.	Joseph's Coat brought to Jacob.
Adam and Eve Hiding.	Joseph and Potiphar.
The Flight from Paradise.	Potiphar's Wife.
The First Labour.	Joseph Accused.
Cain and Abel's Offering.	Joseph in Prison.
The First Murder.	Pharaoh's Baker and Butler.
The Punishment of Cain.	Pharaoh's Dream.
The Command to Noah.	Pharaoh's Indecision.
The Ark.	Joseph before Pharaoh.
The Vineyard of Noah.	Joseph as Ruler.
Noah's Drunkenness.	Joseph's Brethren.
The Building of Babel.	The Cup placed in Benjamin's Sack.
Angels Appearing to Abraham.	The Discovery of the Cup.
Abraham Entertaining the Angels.	His Brethren before Joseph.
The Destruction of the Cities of the Plain.	Jacob on his way to Egypt.
Lot's Escape.	Joseph and his Brethren pleading.
Abraham and Isaac.	Joseph protecting his Brethren.
The Sacrifice of Isaac.	Moses on Sinai.
Isaac and Jacob.	The Miracle of the Red Sea.
Esau and Isaac.	The Destruction of the Egyptians.
Rebecca and Jacob.	Moses striking the Rock.
Jacob and Rachel.	The Law declared.

Was there no humour when such reliefs were carved? Was it only an age of piety and toil, when the poverty of masons and peasants allowed of little jesting? The answer, of course, is that it was the age of the maypole and the Fool, when the wise man reckoned humour as a boon conferred by God, and the bishop found no sin in the smile provoked in church. That is why the decorative heads beneath these Biblical scenes denote laughter as well as fear, though certainly the humour of some is uncomfortably sardonic.

The bosses on the roof are no less varied. One group of figures appears to represent the apothecaries, musicians and armourers whose guilds probably subscribed towards the building costs, but others reveal grotesque monsters emerging from foliage. To some people, the finest sculpture of all is that above the doorway. The arch itself is beautiful. Over it is a bas-relief of Christ, flanked by cherubim and angels, and in the voussoirs of the arch are fourteen small niches with scenes equalling or surpassing those of the arcade in execution and power. Their subjects are vivacious.

In this Battle of the Virtues against the Vices we are able to be interested spectators. We see Generosity pouring coin down the throat of Avarice, Temperance pouring liquor into the mouth of Intemperance, Fortitude trampling on Terror who cuts her own throat, Faith stamping on Infidelity, Truth pulling out Falsehood's tongue, Modesty scourging Lust, and Virtue covering a Vice with her cloak and being stabbed as a reward. These allegories were favoured by artists of the period—at Canterbury they were incised on the pavement around the shrine of Thomas à Becket. What distinguishes these at Salisbury and raises them to the highest class of art is their intensity of life and movement. Men accustomed to pick their words have ranked them as the finest examples extant, just as other people think of the chapter house itself as the most inspiring of the Cathedral's buildings, but in these matters each man should be his own arbiter.

For most of us, the choice is difficult. Salisbury's treasures are almost inexhaustible. Those in the Library alone fill a bulky catalogue, and a brief selection of them hardly does justice to the rest. Of course, the contemporary copy of Magna Carta must be viewed, though it is not so elaborately written as the copy at Lincoln. Naturally, the antiquarian, the calligraphist and the historian must examine the letters of Henry III (1232) and Edward I (1285), and the licence granted by Edward III at Nottingham in 1327 for the dean and chapter to crenellate the close. There are also 187 volumes of manuscripts, many of them beyond the dreams of collectors.

Among them are an early twelfth-century edition of the Confessions of St. Augustine, in thirteen books ; many tracts and extracts from the writings of saints, dating from the same period; a benedictional of the thirteenth century, scrolled in a fine bold hand; early grammatical works ; a large vellum with double columns, of the early fourteenth century, bequeathed " at the price of 13s. 4d." by Henry de la Wyle, Chancellor from 1313 to 1327 ; manuscripts with initials of gold and rich colours, and others, alas, with the initials cut out. Here is the Venerable Bede, the writing dating from the eleventh to twelfth centuries. There are even earlier works. From tenth-century France is a psalter with the Gallician and Hebrew versions side by side in double columns, ornamented with lustrous initials of intricate designs set about with pendant leaves or shaped like fishes. There is a Gallician psalter, probably dating from the year 970, its initials mainly depicting dragons or birds and coloured a dusky red, though the smaller initials of the verses are picked out with green and yellow. There is a breviary giving the service of the boy bishop, and a solemn chant beginning : " Remember youre promys made yn baptism."

Perhaps the most prized possessions of all are Chaucer's translation of the Confessions of Boethius, and early printed books, bearing such impressive dates as 1473 and 1481. Some of the vellum has been damaged by damp ; some of the leaves of the ancient books have been torn away. Enough remains to make the collector's eyes glisten and to arouse the interest of the intelligent layman, though it would be a pity to be too engrossed to glance through the windows at the cloister below.

Centuries ago, old Leland had an agreeable word for the cloister. It was, he said, "one of the largest and most magnificentist in Britain". In shape an exact square, its long covered walks on all sides afford a constant picture of the green sward of the garth, shadowed by the two spreading trees and inset with tiny plates which denote graves. In this enclosure of cool grey stone the solitude is peculiarly restful. From one corner the library, which forms a low storey on the southern gallery, is seen with the chapter house behind it, and here the view suggests that one is looking at a castle with particularly fine windows.

From any angle, the effect is a combination of dignity and delicacy. Along the four galleries are forty-four bays, separated by buttresses, open towards the garth and with a blind archway against the enclosure wall. The shafts separating the open bays were once of Purbeck marble, but they had to be replaced by stone nearly a century ago, and in design conform to the general pattern of the Cathedral. Each noble arch envelops two smaller ones, separated by a four-shafted pier, and these in turn are divided by a single shaft. It cannot be denied that the arcade above the arches is plain and perhaps too high for perfect balance, but the lovely contours of the arches, as well as the size and symmetry of the cloister as a whole, surely justify Leland's arch-superlative of "magnificentist".

Another unusual, more homely word, belongs to the narrow, lengthy court between the cloister and the Cathedral—the Plumberies. That suggests foresight by the medieval builders. Evidently they realized that the great building would need renovations and repairs from time to time, and therefore allowed room for materials and workmen. Past the door of this court, over the gravestones with which the galleries' floor is inlaid, one returns to the Cathedral's nave for a final appreciation of an incomparable vista.

> As many days as in the year there be,
> So many windows in this church we see ;
> As many marble pillars here appear
> As there are hours throughout the fleeting year ;
> As many gates as moons one year does view—
> Strange tale to tell ! Yet not more strange than true.

So runs the local rhyme, but Salisbury's claim is a higher one than that of an almanac in architecture. Nor is its "cool beauty" the last impression which every visitor carries away. There is a preponderance of dark blue and ruby in the windows. There is a profusion of flowers against the grey freestone and darker marble, so that in late summer the nave is brightened by golden rod, the graceful spikes of buddleia, pink phlox and marigolds arranged in brass vases. The soft blue of scabious is set against a warrior's tomb and fuchsia on the grave of a bishop who died half a thousand years ago. In the secluded choir, beside the silver crucifix, are white phlox and a sheaf of gladioli. Gold and crimson and green are reflected from the effigies of saints and soldiers. There are such jewels in stone as the canopied tomb of Giles de Bridport, the lovely Perpendicular arches, the cenotaph of Richard le Poore.

Architecturally, there are the splendid unity, symmetry and simplicity manifest in the Cathedral's design.   In feeling, here is the supreme expression of the Early English style, varied by fine examples of such later periods as the Decorated and the Perpendicular. Though the abundance of Purbeck marble endows the long nave with an appearance of austerity and coolness, the merest glint of sunshine through the tall lancet windows transforms the scene to one of lightness and warmth; when the nave is bathed in full sunlight the effect from the choir is of almost dazzling brilliance.   So much for the visual interests of a great achievement in stone.   As an engineering feat, the building is a triumph. The methods by which the walls were raised on soft soil, and the enormous weight of the tower and spire added without disaster, bespeak the ingenuity as well as the determination of the Gothic innovators.

Historically, the Cathedral is a bridge between the Roman and Reformed Churches. In olden days, many indulgences were granted to worshippers who prayed at the tombs of Giles de Bridport, William Longespee and Bishop Nicholas Longespee, the period of indulgence ranging from thirteen to forty days.   Or the devout might gain indulgence by praying for the souls of the Earl of Lincoln, Chancellor Ralph of York, and various canons and vicars.   By such means too, money was raised—for though the builders were rich, their pockets were not illimitable.   To sinners who contributed to the fabric of the Cathedral, the Archbishop of Canterbury relaxed forty days' penance.   You may see his edict, bearing his seal and the counterseal of St. Thomas, and you may find a similar document issued by the Bishop of Llandaff.

These practices ended with the last bishop of the old order, the Cardinal Lorenzo Campeggio who appears in Shakespeare's *Henry VIII* as Campeius.   Though deprived of his see by Henry's thunderbolt, he was regarded by Rome as Bishop of Salisbury until his death.   To emphasize this violent change in the country's religion, you may turn to the " Petition of the Inhabitants of the Close of the Canons of Sarum to the Field Marshall Generall of His Majesties Western Forces ", praying that the city's defence should not be commanded by a " Romish serjeaunte major ".

Salisbury's great Church, surviving revolutions both spiritual and temporal, unharmed by the vibrations of motor traffic and the explosions of bombs, has triumphed over Time. Or rather, shall we say, the repose it conveys is timeless.   In the final analysis, its highest merit is not the possession of this treasure or that, not even its matchless examples of a style of architecture in which strength was combined with refinement.   The whole edifice imparts a sense of peace beyond the petty measurement of days and years, and a beauty that was inspired.

Moreover, the feeling of repose is not quickly numbed by leaving the nave through the famous west porch and returning to the close.   Again one observes the tranquil setting of " smooth-shaven lawns," the fine trees around Choristers' Green and the Bishop's Walk, with dignified buildings beyond—the Bishop's Palace, the gabled King's House that is said to date from the fourteenth century, the picturesque and lovely Deanery, the School and the Bishop's Wardrobe.   Enough remains of the medieval aspect for us to admire with old Leland " the large embatelid waulle of the palace ", and the soft flowing

Avon is still a restful delight in a noisy world.   Though the city is busy and not without noise, for it has a flourishing trade and is not content to be only a cathedral town, it is no disgrace to the Cathedral.   The old Poultry Cross still stands, variously ascribed to John de Montacute, Earl of Salisbury, or to Lawrence de St. Martin, one of whom committed the sacrilege of carrying home the Sacramental bread and eating it for his supper, for which he was condemned to " set up a cross in Salisbury market place and come every Saturday of his life in shirt and breeches and there confess his fault publickly".   A church founded by Richard le Poore in or about the year 1226 has interest not entirely banished by his greater creation.   A fine medieval hall, home of a rich wool merchant who built it in 1470, has a stone fireplace and a magnificent oaken screen in its banqueting chamber. . . .   In these respects Salisbury is fortunate ; it is not overshadowed by the cathedral but accords with it.   Yet it is impossible to think of the city without thinking also of the masterpiece to which it owed its birth.

Foreign artists of old burst into tears on first seeing the Cathedral, " grieving that they had not the like in their own land", said a church historian who lived in Shakespeare's time.   Later artists, it may be, were more restrained, but lesser painters than Constable have realized that the building and spire and trees offer a perfect composition.   Nor does a man need to be an artist to recognize the symmetry of design, a stonemason to appreciate the splendour of detail, a schoolmaster its history, or a cleric its high purpose.   The centuries have not tarnished its splendour ; it has seen churches dissolved and kings overthrown, the rise of industrialism and the march of science, the growth of knowledge, the passing of heresies and the advent of strange new evils.   It remains a glory and a wonder no less than when men fought with arrows and lived in squalor.   " She stands and still shall stand ; she remains and shall remain ; a watcher of the generations."

LIST OF THE PLATES

LIST OF THE PLATES (contd.)

The tranquil River Avon in the foreground, an ancient house and stately trees, and the spire of the Cathedral rising behind them.   Man and Nature have together formed a perfect composition for the artist.

From the Bishop's Palace, the symmetry of the Cathedral can be appreciated at a glance. Nave, transepts, choir—each is an integral part of the design, and the Decorated spire harmonizes with the earlier style of the main building.

Few buttresses were required to bear the weight of the spire. The towers of other cathedrals collapsed under a similar strain, but the thirteenth-century builders of the main structure had worked well on the soft valley soil.

The west front is famous for its lavish decoration and the trinity of superb Early English windows. Though somewhat crowded in effect, its opulence contrasts effectively with the simplicity of the rest of the exterior.

Figures of saints, martyrs and virgins stand on ornamented pedestals in the eleven narrow niches above the west door. The originals were destroyed by the Puritans, and were not replaced until the middle of the nineteenth century.

Though the doorway is not impressive in size, the lovely arch is embellished with rich moulding and capitals.   It
carries a representation of St. Mary (to whom the Cathedral is dedicated) and the Holy Child.

43

Still closer inspection of the west front porch reveals the care which the masons devoted to detail—the bases and capitals of the Purbeck marble piers, the bosses of the fluted arches, and even to the setting of plain stone blocks.

The severe beauty of the north entrance is perfectly framed by the tree-studded lawn of the close.   This porch was
built soon after 1220 ; the west front was added thirty or forty years later.

The spire is still braced inside by the original timber scaffolding.   Outside, these metal bands were strapped round
the base of the tower by Sir Christopher Wren when subsidence threatened to split the masonry.

46

Wren's metal straps can be seen again in this view of the tower from the chapter house. Little, however, has had to be done to the structure, which continues to astonish architects by its audacious engineering.

Much of the excellent workmanship cannot be appreciated from the ground. The fine coping, the buttresses and their graceful pinnacles are witnesses to the skill of the builders of six hundred and seven hundred years ago.

The exterior of the canons' vestry, the muniment room, and the south choir transept. " The building composes perfectly from whatever viewpoint," says a guide-book on the Cathedral; few will disagree.

Above: the cloisters and chapter house; below: another view of the cloisters. These photographs, taken from the roof of the nave, emphasize not only the quality of the architecture but also the Cathedral's beautiful setting.

The east side of the cloisters, which are generally considered to be the largest and finest in Britain. They were
probably planned by Giles de Bridport (1217-62) and completed by later bishops.

Each of the four galleries of the cloisters consists of ten bays separated by buttresses, with an additional bay at each corner—forty-four in all. Open on one side, the cloisters have blind arches set against the enclosure wall.

52

Each lovely arch enfolds two smaller arches separated by a four-shafted pier.   These, in turn, are divided by a single shaft.   The original columns of marble perished and were replaced by stone a century ago.

An exterior of one of the bays emphasizes the supreme artistry of the designer of the cloisters. They were built at a time when the idea of " England " was an inspiration to the nation's leaders and artists.

At whatever point one stands within the cloisters there are views of serene beauty. Here is conveyed the atmosphere of peace which is enclosed by the walls of Salisbury's ancient cloisters.

Inside the nave.   The arches on either side have been described by artists as perfectly shaped.   Four slender shafts of Purbeck marble are clustered round the core of each pier so that strength is combined with gracefulness.

56

From the west window the eye is led from the brightly lit nave to the dimness of the choir and the mystery of the high altar, to the ruby and violet richness of the glass in the Lady Chapel.

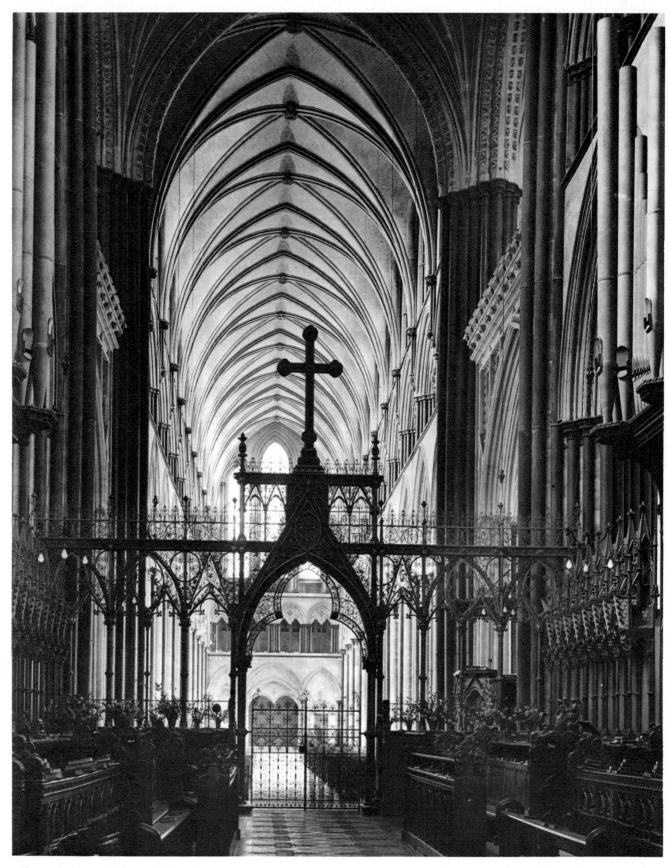

The inspiring brilliance of the nave is all the more apparent when it is seen through the open tracery of the choir screen. The lightness of soft grey freestone is delicately veined by the dark marble shafts and vaulting ribs.

The great west window—" the consummation of Early English art ".   Most of the ancient stained glass, saved from the fanatical despoilers who followed the Reformation, is in its three high lancets, aflame with colour.

The nave aisles harmonize with the design of the nave. But they are much less lofty and the contour of the roof is sharper, giving an impression of seclusion despite the double lancet windows.

Behind the golden blaze of the high altar there are curiously shaped painted arches. For a moment one has the impression of being in a Moorish temple. There is nothing like them in any other English cathedral.

The wealth of decoration on the high altar contrasts with the severity of the Early English columns and the geometrical lines of the Lady Chapel roof. The altar fittings, like the reredos and the bishop's throne, are modern.

62

The enrichment of the high altar is the work of an age whose taste was not of the best. The craftsmanship of the Spanish processional cross which now stands on the altar is, however, of rare excellence.

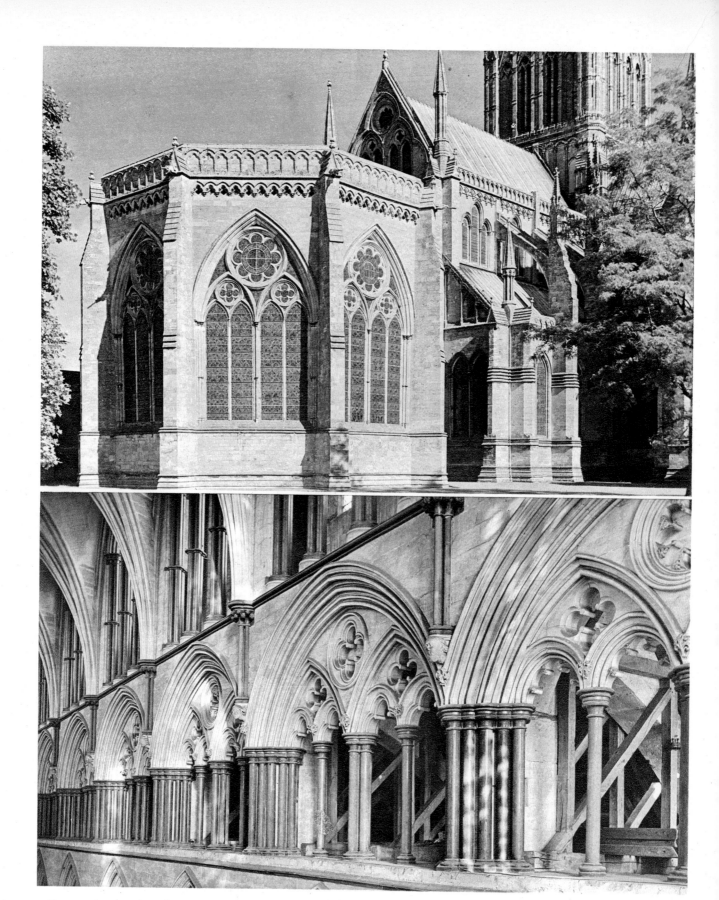

Above: the exterior of the chapter house whose design is of surpassing grace.   Below: the exquisite arches of the triforium whose delicate piers are made of Purbeck marble.

Friends of Salisbury are sure that its chapter house is the most beautiful in the country.   The single arch of the
lovely doorway encloses two smaller arches of cinquefoil outline and carries a bas-relief of the Saviour.

The chapter house is lit by seven huge and magnificent windows, and an eighth smaller one over the entrance. Separated by heavily grouped Purbeck piers, each window enfolds two secondary lights.

The groining of the roof of the chapter house rises gracefully from the central pier, and the ribs terminate on the pilasters between the windows. Round the core of the central pillar are eight shafts of marble.

Around the canopy in the chapter house are six-hundred-years-old high reliefs, famous for their boldness and vigour. Here, from left to right, are those depicting Adam's Labour; the Offerings of Cain and Abel; and the First Murder.

The top picture shows : Creation of the Earth ; Creation of the Sun and Moon ; Creation of Birds and Fishes ; Creation of Beasts and Adam and Eve.   Lower picture :   The Command to Noah ; The Ark ; Noah's Vineyard.

Originally the reliefs in the chapter house were brightly painted.   Top: the Red Sea Miracle and the Destruction of the Egyptians.   Bottom: the Temptation, Adam and Eve Hiding, and the Expulsion from Eden.

Among the sixty scenes are (top) the Seventh Day and the Tree of Good and Evil. Bottom left: only Joseph's feet are visible as he is thrust into the Pit. Right: Jacob Meets Rachel; a three-faced man is carved below.

Part of the original stone choir screen or pulpitum, which separated the choir from the nave, is now in the morning chapel. It was removed by " the unspeakable Wyatt ", who made extensive alterations to the Cathedral in 1789.

The decorative heads in the chapter house beneath the Biblical scenes denote laughter as well as awe, though the humour of some is " uncomfortably sardonic ". The period in which they were carved was that of the jester.

73

The north transept contains three monuments by the English artist, Flaxman, who revived the interest of the western world in sculpture. Two of them are in the Gothic style, and there is also an effigy by Chantrey.

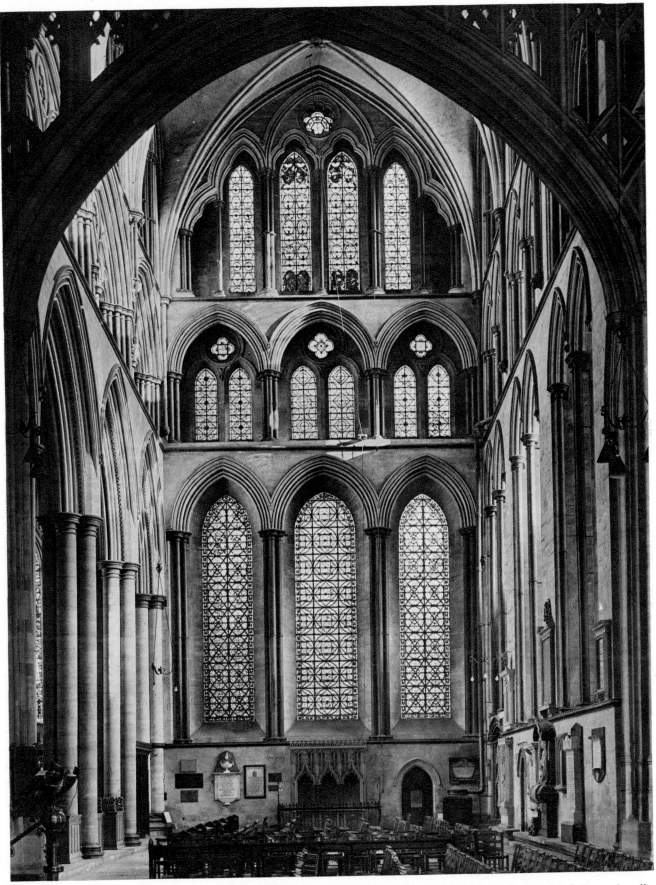

The south transept, brilliantly lit by the lovely recessed windows which occupy the whole width of the end wall. The canopied table tomb, gorgeously decorated, holds the remains of Bishop Mitford who died in 1407.

Top picture : detail of the choir roof, showing the restored medieval medallions which were once obliterated by a colour wash. Lower picture : looking up one of the pillars, bowed under the immense weight of the tower and spire.

76

The wonderful timber strutting inside the spire. Despite the shocks of modern times, tower and spire have not deviated in position for more than a hundred years : a tribute, surely, to the fourteenth-century carpenters and masons.

These are the sturdy supports for the roof of the south transept.   Though never seen by ordinary visitors the Cathedral's timber is no less remarkable than the abundance of magnificently carved freestone and dark marble.

This primitive, drum-like engine stands in the tower.   It was probably used as a treadmill to haul up the blocks of stone when the spire was built six hundred years ago.   The tower consists of two stages or storeys.

The tone of the clock-bells in the tower is particularly fine and full. The ascent to the spire above is so difficult that even the fireguards during the war of 1939-45 rarely went higher than this room.

The staircase to the library shows the severe beauty of the Early English style, in which decoration was subordinate to clarity of line. The library forms a low storey over the eastern gallery of the cloister.

Among the library treasures are a gospel lectionary (seen in the top picture) and a thirteenth-century benedictional (lower picture). In the latter the illuminated initials and the boldness of the lettering are especially notable.

The thirteenth-century chains are a reminder that books were virtually irreplaceable when every copy had to be written laboriously by hand. No fewer than 187 manuscript volumes are in Salisbury's library.

The chantry of Bishop Edmund Audley (1502-1524), as seen from the high altar. Unusual in design it has the richness and delicacy of detail which is associated with the Late Perpendicular style.

Seen from the choir aisle the two bays of the Audley chantry are better harmonized. The decoration is remarkable. The stone is cut into " the intricacy of old lace and seemingly as light as silk ".

In the north transept, next to the tomb of a bishop who died in 1499, is the iron mechanism of the clock which was made in the year 1386 or even earlier. Lower picture: the splendid tomb of Bishop Mitford (d. 1407).

In 1778 a barbarous earl removed the Hungerford chantry from the nave to the choir and converted it into his family pew. Hungerford fought with Henry V at Agincourt. The chantry's ironwork is among the earliest in England.

" An exquisite jewel of stonework, one of the most precious in England "—the chantry of Bishop Giles de Bridport (1217-1262). Scenes from his life are sculptured above the arches ; angels bearing censers support the effigy's head.

The tomb of William Longespée the Elder, who was the first to be buried in the Cathedral. Half-brother of King Richard I and King John, he gained the first English naval victory over the French in 1213.

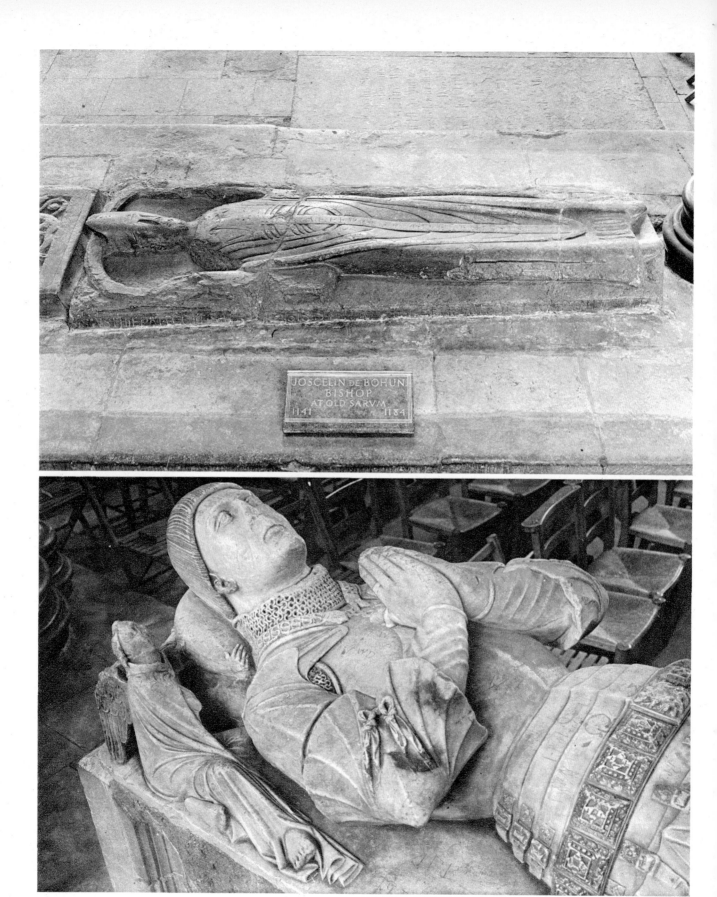

Top picture : the grave of Bishop Jocelyn (died, 1184) which was brought from Old Sarum. Below is the effigy of Robert, Lord Hungerford (died, 1459), notable for the fine armour and the sumptuous belt.

This tomb slab, believed to cover the body of Roger the Justiciar, was also removed from Old Sarum when the " new " Cathedral was built. Roger, statesman-bishop who accumulated a vast fortune, died in 1142.

Above : a full-length view of the fluted armour on Robert, Lord Hungerford's effigy.   Lower picture : the shrine of St. Osmund (died, 1099).   Into its openings sick people used to thrust their limbs in expectation of cure.

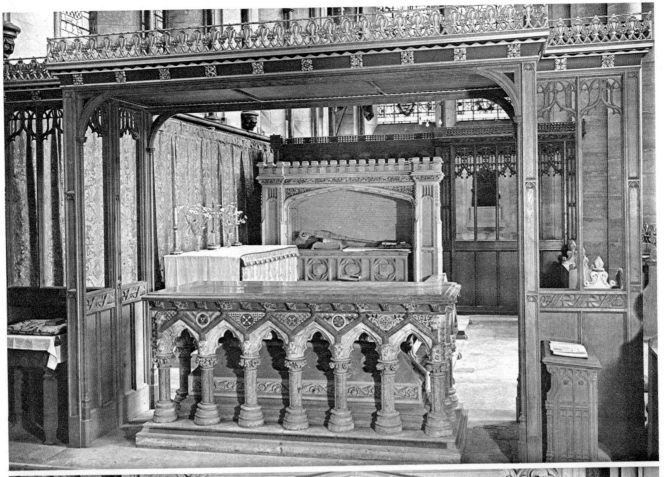

Below: the tomb of Thomas Bennett, precentor from 1542 to 1558, is surmounted by one of the grisly skeleton effigies so favoured in the Middle Ages.   Above: the beautiful chapel in the south transept.

Bishop Guest, who died in 1577, is commemorated by a splendid brass—and by the long inscription in stately Latin. But it will be noticed that the Elizabethan artist refused to flatter the heavy-faced prelate.

In the south aisle is a quaint memorial to the " trulie vertuous and religious " Elihonour Sadler, who died in 1622. The flowery inscription speaks of her " fervent zeale, her Pietie, Sanctitie, Charitie, and continual care of the Poore ".

Near the Lady Chapel is the golden tomb of Edward Seymour, Earl of Hertford, and his wife Catherine, sister to Lady Jane Grey. Queen Elizabeth, angered by Seymour's marriage, imprisoned him and his wife in the Tower.

The south choir aisle is invested with the scarlet and gold of the opulent, seventeenth-century tomb of Sir Richard Mompesson and his wife Katherine. Its surfeit of decoration is characteristic of the Jacobean love of ornament.

97

Next to one of the lovely choir gateways is the Bishop's throne. Further to the right are some of the wonderfully carved wooden stalls ; their seats and elbows date from the late thirteenth century, their poppy-heads from about 1520.

Bench ends in the choir stalls.　　Two hundred years and more ago all the old woodwork was painted in white and gold and blue.　　Defoe said that it resembled " a theatre rather than a venerable Choir of a Church".

The richly gilded chapel of St. Michael in the south transept is dedicated to the memory of men who fell in the first world war. The reredos, or altar screen, is notable for its delicate carving.

Top left : consecration cross outside the south transept.   Right : lavatory, or washing-trough, in the morning chapel.
Bottom left : chequer board in the east cloister walk.   Right : ancient stone coffin in the cloister.

Saints and martyrs on the great west front—top picture : at the north-west corner ; lower picture : at the south-west corner. Carved some seven hundred years ago, the figures are remarkable for their vigour and naturalness.

Boldness is also displayed in the smaller figures, such as the gargoyles seen above. (That on the right has been chosen by birds as a nesting place.) The lower picture shows a gargoyle attended by demons.

These carvings of bishops on the west front of the Cathedral provide an interesting comparison with the brilliantly coloured modern statues illustrated on the opposite page.

Glittering with colour these statues face the south transept. Left: the statue of Elias de Derham, the canon who helped to build the Cathedral. Right: the statue of Bishop le Poore, founder of the Cathedral.

The south-east corner of the close. The memorial cross was erected to the memory of Bishop Fisher, known during his lifetime as " The King's Fisher ", who died in 1825 and was buried at St. George's Chapel, Windsor.

Looking from the north door of the Cathedral across the lawns of the close we see the other end of the road from the North Gate and the High Street.

Rugged, simple but effective, St. John's Gate is one of several entrances to the Cathedral's close.   It was in 1326 that Edward III granted a licence for the building of an embattled wall round the close.

Much of the stone used to build the wall (lower picture) was brought from the ruins of Old Sarum.   Around the lovely
North Gate (top picture) there are traces of Norman carving on the masonry.

Set round the great church are the Bishop's Palace, the Deanery and gabled King's House, the Bishop's Wardrobe and—on the north side—these charmingly varied houses.   In summer their tiny gardens glow with flowers and shrubs.

Approaching by the finely arched North Gate, " the little houses and shops seem to suggest centuries of uneventful life". At first, only the spire can be glimpsed, but presently the whole vast length of the Cathedral unfolds to the gaze.

Time and again Constable, England's greatest landscape painter, was inspired by the view of river and church. No other cathedral in England has such symmetry of design, and none a more spacious or more tranquil setting.

From the old water mill, Salisbury's spire rises from the trees like " a tall finger pointing to Perfection "—the crown of a building that for seven hundred years has been a glory and an inspiration in stone.

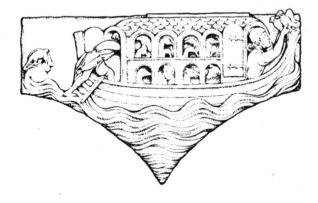

A GLOSSARY OF ARCHITECTURAL AND ECCLESIASTICAL TERMS

Abacus : The slab constituting the top member of a capital.

Ambulatory : A walk ; especially the aisle enclosing an apse.

Apse : A semi-circular recess.

Arabesque : An intertwined style of ornamentation.

Arcade : A series of arches.

Ashlar : Stonework of a regular, square shape.

Aumbry : A receptacle for alms ; a small niche with a door.

Ball-flower : A stone or wood enrichment, common in fourteenth-century architecture.

Bay : A section of wall between buttresses ; a wall recess or arched opening.

Benedictional : A prayer-book.

Boss : A prominence, knob or stud ; an ornamental protuberance of a ceiling.

Buttress : Stonework built against a wall to strengthen it.

Capital : The upper section of a pillar.

Chancel : The eastern part of a church containing the altar.

Chantry : A chapel endowed for the daily celebration of mass for the soul of one deceased.

Cinquefoil : An ornamentation resembling five leaves.

Clerestory : The windowed upper part of a church above the roofs of the aisles.

Consistory court : An ecclesiastical court or assembly.

Corbel : A projection from a wall, generally of stone.

Crocket : An ornamentation placed at intervals on the sides of a gable.

Cusp : A projecting curve ; especially in tracery.

Drip-stone : The outer moulding of an arch. (Also label.)

Enrichment : Recurring ornamentation on a moulding.

Feretory : A repository for shrines.

Finial : An ornamentation at the top of a gable, pinnacle, and the like.

Flying buttress : An open-arched support built from pier to wall.

Foliate : To ornament with leaf-like carvings.

Groin : The angle at the intersection of roof vaultings.

Justiciar : One who dispenses the law.

Label : The outer moulding of an arch. (Also drip-stone.)

Lancet : An Early English window with a pointed head.

Lectionary : A mass-book containing the epistles and gospels to be read at services.

Lierne : One of a number of short ribs supporting the vault and knitting the main arch-ribs together, which in turn transfer the weight to the shafts beneath.

Misericord or *Miserere :* A seat in a choir stall, hinged, often with carvings on the underside.

Moulding : A projecting line of stone.

Nave : The body of a church (from the west front to the chancel).

Ogee : (Of an arch.) A compound arch shaped somewhat like the letter S—that is, with a concave and a convex curve.

Pier : A supporting pillar ; a wall section between windows.

Pilaster : A pillar set partly in a wall.

Piscina : A receptacle set in a niche at the side of an altar to receive the water used during a service.

Prebendary : An ecclesiastic holding the living of a canon.

Pulpitum : A stone screen dividing monastic cathedrals into two parts : the east, for the rituals of the Order ; the west, for public services and the devotions of pilgrims.

Purbeck marble : A grey or greenish limestone quarried from the stone strata which runs from Purbeck in Dorset to the Yorkshire coast.

Quatrefoil : An ornamentation resembling four leaves.

Rebus : An enigmatic illustration of a name, suggesting its syllables.

Reredos : An ornamental screen set behind and above an altar.

Retrochoir : That part of a church to the rear of the high altar.

Return stalls : Stalls in the chancel facing the high altar.

Roodloft : A gallery above the carved screen dividing nave and choir.

Shaft : That part of a pillar between base and capital.

Spandrel : The surface enclosed by the outer curve of an arch and its surrounding framework.

String course : A horizontal line of mouldings in a wall.

Suffragan : An assistant bishop of a diocese.

Transept : The transverse arms of a cruciform church.

Trefoil : An ornamentation resembling three leaves.

Triforium : The gallery above the aisles.

Tympanum : The surface over a doorway or window enclosed by the lintel and a surmounting arch.

Undercroft : A vault.

Voussoir : One of the stones or bricks of which an arch is formed.

A Plan of
SALISBURY CATHEDRAL

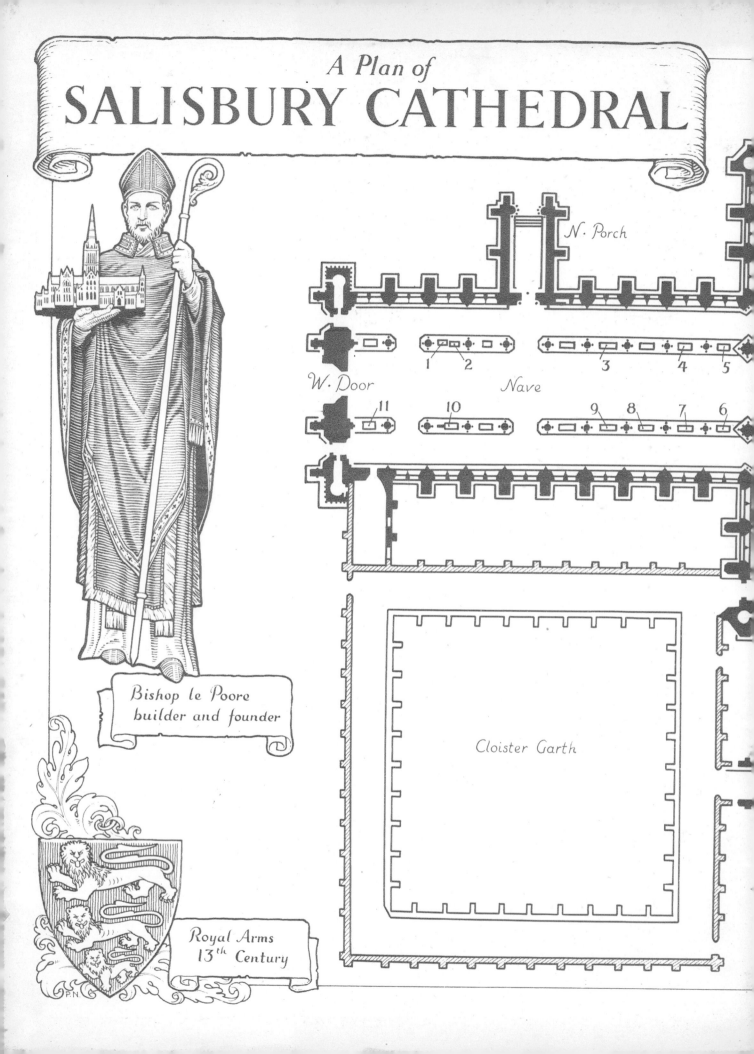

N. Porch

W. Door

Nave

1 2   3   4 5

11 10   9 8 7 6

Cloister Garth

Bishop le Poore
builder and founder

Royal Arms
13th Century